The First Good News

Protoevangelium

Genesis 3:15

And I will put enmity

Between you and the woman,

And between your seed and her Seed;

He shall bruise your head,

And you shall bruise His heel.

To Shelia

You are always my best girl and fellowship of the Gospel.

To Lily,

Thank you for being faithful to the Lord and my muse for this book.

To my son, Dillon Cameron Jackson,

May the Lord watch over me and you while we are apart. I am looking forward to the day that I see the true you. I thank the Lord for giving you mercy and letting you rest until the day we meet again.

Rest in Peace

June 14, 1994 - February 18, 2022

Cover design by A. Cameron Jackson

Published 2022 by DeepRichDirt Publishing

www.DeepRichDirt.com

DeepRichDirt Publishing presents

Religion & Philosophy Shelf

As with all our books — particularly works of adult nonfiction — the viewpoints expressed in these pages are those of the author. DeepRichDirt Publishing seeks to broadly promote a free culture by facilitating an open marketplace of ideas, both old and new. We find value in presenting and examining various concepts, both our own and others'. This is why we seek, over time, to provide a wealth of diverse viewpoints to readers, giving voice to a rich collection of unique authors. Following basic principles of love and honesty, we hope this and each other book in the Religion & Philosophy Shelf holds potential to enrich a person or a community somewhere.

For communications regarding the content of this book, please feel free to contact the author directly at acameronjackson@gmail.com.

CONTENTS

Foreword by Dr. Jeff Hoglen 5

Introduction 8

Acknowledgments 37

Chapter 1 The Beginning of the Universe 40

Chapter 2 The Beginning of Life 54

Chapter 3 The Beginning of Sin and Curse 68

Chapter 4 The Beginning of the Effects of Sin 86

Chapter 5 The Beginning of the Age of Man 94

Chapter 6 The Beginning of Judgement 101

Chapter 7 The Beginning of the Global Flood 114

Chapter 8 The Beginning of a New World 127

Chapter 9 The Beginning of Covenants 139

Chapter 10 The Beginning of Nations 157

Chapter 11 The Tower of Confusion 166

Chapter 12 The Good News According to the Beloved Apostle 175

Chapter 13 The Good News According to Jesus 192

Chapter 14 The Good News You can Share 199

FOREWORD BY DR. JEFF HOGLEN

It has been my pleasure to know Cameron Jackson for the past few years in a friendship that has gone from acquaintance to co-laborer within the ministry. Since he and Shelia came with their daughter Lily to RockFish Church in Raeford, NC, I have watched him grow in his relationship with Jesus to the place where his heart burns with the desire to go deeper into the realm of apologetics. I have watched his family live out the meaning of "life on mission" with all of them entrenched in both church outreach activities and personal evangelism – life on life.

Cameron has a passion for apologetics, and it shows. There is a difference between a theorist and a practitioner. Cameron is the latter. He takes his knowledge of apologetics and uses it every day. I have known him to go onto college campuses and start conversations with students, then tactfully share the truths of the Gospel and why the Bible can be trusted.

This book is for everyone from seeker to lifelong follower of Christ. Cameron gives careful thought and explains his points in such a way that it's not overwhelming but still chock-full of substance. Along the way, he dispenses his brand of humor, which can be helpful when tackling such an important subject.

I heard someone say, "Reading one hour per day in your chosen field will make you an international expert in seven years." If this is true (and I believe it is), then Cameron Jackson is an expert within the field of apologetics. He has put in the time, and the results are now in your hand. His proclivity for this subject has opened many doors. He has been featured on Alex McFarland's Truth For A New Generation radio program and has also been a part of his most recent apologetics tour.

I am happy to call him a friend and wholeheartedly recommend this book. Get your highlighters ready; this is going to be a great read!

Dr. Jeff Hoglen, D.Min

CEO - Churchplanting.com

Teaching Pastor – RockFish Church

INTRODUCTION

1

As I remember back to that day in 1985, my preparation to visit my mother was an exciting moment. Mom and Dad had been separated for a few months. My father and I were going to make that five-hour drive straight through without stopping. I had promised my mother this trip would be the last trip for me. I wasn't going to come back to Houston, where I was living at the time. I was going to take care of her and my brothers because being separated from her was taking a toll on me; I even had a plan to start a painting business in Picayune, Mississippi.

My mother and I spoke on Christmas Eve, finalizing our plan for me to move there permanently. My mother and father had separated because my father was an alcoholic and had physically abused her. However, that is another story for another time. Now we will relive the moment that changed my life.

It must have been a chilly predawn January morning. My mom and brothers, three-year-old Junior and three-month-old Larry, were sleeping inside a friend's home in Picayune, Mississippi. In the space between the living room couch and the wall, an electrical arc fault sparked silently to life, causing a fire to emerge. It was probably a newly built house, with drywall that still smelled of fresh paint. The fire began to spread from within the walls into the living room, causing flames to spread throughout the house. To better understand the circumstances, let us trace the story back a little.

As I heard the story from my brother, it began like this.

Sylvia, friend and homeowner, screamed, “My goodness! The house is on fire!”

Everett, owner, raced from the bedroom as flames built up, shouting. “Everyone get out, get out now!”

He wanted everyone to escape out of the house. The fire was creeping from the living room to the bedrooms from inside the walls. It was spreading into the kitchen and the hallways. Everyone woke up and rushed out into the backyard in a panic situation.

My mom was startled by the screaming and yelling of everyone around her, and then she proceeded to get out of the home, only to realize that her children were still inside the guest room sleeping. Without hesitation, my mom bravely fought the fire and rushed inside to rescue her babies, Junior and Larry. By this time the fire and smoke were raging. It was thickened to black as the flames moved to the kitchen.

The house’s layout was not simple. The hallway was narrow, and the bedrooms seemed a long way into the tunnel of smoke. She must have choked on smoke as she forced her way to the bedroom at the end of the hallway. By the time Mom reached the entrance of the guest bedroom door, her hair and face were burning. This information was given to me by the fire marshal and the mortician. She gave up her life and lay between her two precious boys as she took her last painful breath.

Everyone tried to stop her from entering the fire-raging home, but there's no stopping a mother's bond to rescue her babies. I am very sure her courage has earned her a badge of honor at the judgement seat of God.

John 15:13. Greater love has no one than this, than to lay down one's life for his friends.

My mother died on January 29, 1985. My brother, Junior and Larry, also died the same night. Their death is the most heart-breaking, devastating, shocking, tearful, life-affirming, and spiritually-love-filled experience I have ever had. I have added "spiritually-love-filled" because I did not want to sound like I needed sympathy, but because I believe that this is something that as human beings, we need to talk about more.

The horrible way that my mother and brothers had to die was not easy to bear, and it was a feeding ground for spiritual hate to feast upon. Satan was knocking on my mind, causing havoc with my mental wellbeing. In the bathroom in my apartment, I contemplated taking my life.

I remember reading about Charles Darwin's biography, in which Annie's cruel death destroyed Charles's belief and chimed the final death-knell for his Christianity. Charles Darwin took a stand as an unbeliever. Another example is the story of Ted Turner, who became an obnoxious unbeliever because Mary Jane, his sister, died of a painful disease called systemic lupus erythematosus. Turner exclaimed, "And I couldn't understand how someone so innocent should be made or allowed to suffer so." He blamed God for his tragic loss.

That night, I prayed the prayer of Job for God to be bigger than my suffering and to give me the power of the Holy Spirit to overcome my grief. When it comes to the Bible, I was knowledgeable because since the age of 10 I have read it. Although my theology was skewed due to being a Jehovah's Witness, I knew the context of the scriptures. In that small, confined bathroom, I began to open my New King James Bible.

I remember reading:

Job 1:20. Then Job arose, tore his robe, and shaved his head; and he fell to the ground and worshiped. 21. And he said:

"Naked I came from my mother's womb,

And naked shall I return there.

The Lord gave, and the Lord has taken away;

Blessed be the name of the Lord."

22. In all this Job did not sin nor charge God with wrong.

I would like to point out that the Lord had been ministering to me through my friend Terry, whom I worked with. Just to be clear, I've always been well-versed in the Bible from my early childhood. As early as 10 years old, my grandmother whom I call "Oma" would take me to the neighborhood Protestant church. She would also tell me Bible stories.

I have always had a curiosity for the "truth". As one great man once said, I have promised my God that I would leave no stone unturned in my pursuit of truth. Although I must confess that I have taken some wild and crazy detours, I believe God was leading me to the knowledge of the sound truth that is within the scriptures.

After counting the cost, I began my slow and intentional conversion that led up to one Thursday night in February 1985.

Luke 14:28. For which of you, intending to build a tower, does not sit down first and count the cost, whether he has enough to finish it.

Although the Lord gifted me salvation that night, my open confession was made during a Sunday service at Word Ministry Fellowship led by my pastor, Villard Hunter. It was a glorious day. The joy of my salvation was transparent to everyone around me; nothing seemed to be of importance except for praising and worshiping the Lord.

A few months later, I was baptized in a pool at a friend's house, confirming my inner-heart change with my outwardly expression of my faith. It was not long after that I experienced the baptism of the Holy Spirit while praying in the early morning. Our church was undergoing a prayer revival in which the congregations would gather every morning for one hour.

Matthew 26:40. Then He came to the disciples and found them sleeping, and said to Peter, "What! Could you not watch with Me one hour? 41. Watch and pray, lest you enter into temptation. The spirit indeed is willing, but the flesh is weak."

Every morning we gathered inside the church, praying for our various needs. It was during one of the prayer sessions that the Lord spoke to both Chuck Olsen and me to begin my discipleship training. The Olsens opened their home to me, and I began my discipleship. I have learned so much from this godly man and his family. The process of discipleship strengthened me so much that the Lord gave me another responsibility. The Lord pressed upon my heart by revealing this scripture.

Acts 9:15. But the Lord said to him, "Go, for he is a chosen vessel of Mine to bear My name before Gentiles, kings, and the children of Israel."

Being obedient to God, I entered into "Great Commission Ministry" with two friends, Jeff and Charles. The three of us preached the Gospel of Jesus Christ to the poor, homeless, prostitutes, and homosexuals living on the street of Montrose in Houston, TX. We spent many nights and into the morning ministering to those who would listen, and many were led to the Lord as the Holy Spirit convicted their hearts.

In 1987, the Lord put a burden in my heart to join the military. After boot camp and airborne school, I was stationed in Fort Bragg, North Carolina. Whether I was in the jungle of Panama or the sands of Iraq and Turkey, I kept the word of God close to my heart, literally and figuratively. I always had my pocket Bible in the left pocket of my uniform.

Life in the army was tough, and my spiritual walk with the Lord suffered greatly. The many overseas deployments caused me to lose focus on my salvation walk with the Lord. I suffered from traumatic depression and began to consume alcohol along with cigarettes to cope with my problems. I began to lose the joy of my salvation, and I suffered the consequences of my lack of faith.

It was in 1989 that I met my first wife, Lynette, and we had two children, Ayrielle and Dillon. Although the Lord kept me from harm to my physical body during my time in the army, my spiritual health was deteriorating. It didn't help the matter when the church I attended was lacking the spiritual zeal; in other words, it was a dead church. My marriage broke, and I began to depend upon alcohol to cope with my depression and anxieties.

During the 1990s to early 2000, my spirituality was dead. God stopped speaking to me! I married a non-believer, resulting in a divorce months later. I began to wake from my slumber during the end of my last deployment in 2006, Operation Enduring Freedom. When I returned from my deployment, I found that my wife had taken everything that I owned and left me with an empty house. I began to humble myself before the Lord and asked Him to restore my soul. I cried and pleaded for God's forgiveness.

Psalms 51:11. Do not cast me away from Your presence, And do not take Your Holy Spirit from me.

12. Restore to me the joy of Your salvation, And uphold me by Your generous Spirit.

13. Then I will teach transgressors Your ways, And sinners shall be converted to You.

My knees were beginning to swell from the hours spent trying to crawl my way back to God's grace and mercy in my prayer closet. With the discipline learned from the army, I studied my Bible and the Lord began to open my spiritual eyes again. With a regimen of daily devotions, prayers, and church attendance, I began to feel the love of God in my life.

In 2008, the Lord began to quicken my heart to refocus my life and walk closer to Him than ever before. I began to open my Bible, and God revealed Himself to me. The Lord blessed me with a new wife, Shelia, and a precious child named Lily in 2010. The Word of God is life to my family and me. We study the scriptures to understand and hear what God has planned for us daily. The Lord God almighty has indeed restored unto me the joy of His salvation. Our family entered into ministry in 2017, and we are growing steadily in the Lord.

What is The First Good News?

The first news is found within Genesis 3:15, where by the curse given to the serpent, God revealed to us that He will give us victory over Satan through His son Jesus Christ our savior.

Genesis 3:15. "And I will put enmity between you and the woman, And between your seed and her Seed; He shall bruise your head, And you shall bruise His heel."

This book will expound on this within chapter three, but one can stand upon the promise that God has given us victory in Jesus Christ. God's redemptive plan has begun in Genesis 3:21 and will continue with the coming of the Lord and Savior Jesus.

Genesis 3:21. Also for Adam and his wife the Lord God made tunics of skin, and clothed them.

God's redemptive plan is this. There will be a Savior, which is the seed of the woman, who will be the One that will conquer Satan and therefore conquer sin. Even though He will be bruised while conquering, He will crush the deadly enemy. We will be victorious through Jesus Christ, our Lord and savior. We will have fellowship with God forever in the new heavens and new earth. Let us pray.

Our Father in heaven, we believe in your redemptive plan for salvation which you laid out since the foundation of this world. We are grateful that you have sent your son, Jesus Christ our Lord, to die for us on the cross for our sins over two thousand years ago. We believe Jesus Christ conquered death when you resurrected Him three days later. By this we can hold onto the promise that we will have life, and life eternal. We give you the honor and praise forever in Jesus' name we pray, amen.

2

As the day ends, nine o'clock marks bedtime hour for our family. We all usually prepare to gather in my daughter's room to have some family devotion time. It is during this time that our family converses about matters of the heart. My daughter has just turned ten and she has a heightened curiosity.

One evening, her inquiring mind began to formulate a question that led me to begin a conversation that I didn't expect to explore until she was much older. I know what you're presuming, but this is not exactly the moment that you are thinking about.

The conversation began with an innocent question. "Poppa, I read that Jesus said He was the light, the way, and the truth; I know what He means about the light and even the way, but what is the truth?" She asked me with a sincere curiosity.

At the time, I was engaged in Master of Apologetics studies through Answers in Genesis. Also, I have been listening, reading, and following many apologist teachings and books for a number of years now. However, that night recent articles that I read seemed to come to mind: "Point of Exclusion" and "Think Again" by Ravi Zacharias.

My reply was that truth by definition is exclusive. Everything cannot be true. If everything is true, then nothing is false. The scriptures' clarity or perspicuity must be the presupposition of the truth. If there's the truth then there must be a source of truth, and

I am convinced that the Bible is that source, not because it states it but because Jesus said it.

And then I added further explanation to be sure that she understood the truth I was conveying: "If your worldview is truthful then it would answer four necessary questions: origin, meaning, morality, and destiny. These answers must be correspondingly true on particular questions and, as a whole, all answers put together must be coherent. The three tests for truth must be applied to any worldview: logical consistency, empirical adequacy, and experiential relevance. The Christian message is utterly unique and meets the demand for truth." Of course, the idea is borrowed from renowned apologist Ravi Zacharias.

As I finished the last words on the thoughtfully constructed explanation, I began to sway back in confidence that my daughter would be satisfied with the answer. Instead, her reply was on the contrary.

"I don't understand it, Poppa. Those are too big of words; it is confusing." She continued to say, "Can you give me some example, so I could understand it better."

It was that moment when I realized what I needed to do, how I needed to approach this thing they call apologetics or evangelism—which to me is two sides of one coin. I must keep it simple, but phrase it in such a way that brings out the clarity of the Bible.

Matthew 19:14. But Jesus said, "Let the little children come to Me, and do not forbid them; for of such is the kingdom of heaven."

The meaning is that without the simple faith of a child we cannot enter the kingdom of heaven. My epiphany was clear; I have to break down the Christian worldview to such a degree that a 10-year-old would be able to understand. The philosophy of the truth of Jesus should be simple because the scripture makes it simple. If the gospel is truly simple, then our Christian worldview should be simple enough that even a 10-year-old can understand and be able to grasp the concept.

As I thought about this approach to apologetics, my mind began to formulate a strategy or a way to explain the concept of the Christian worldview. It is very crucial that Christian leaders employ simple techniques to explain, expound and make sense of what is the Christian worldview for the next generation. This process has to include the love of Jesus Christ, our Savior.

Many of us have seen the slogan *Jesus is the answer*; but many more people are asking what the question is. I believe the gospel of Jesus Christ is beautiful and unique in its perspective and approach, but more importantly it is true. Telling the truth is inherently easy, yet we make it so complicated. We make the gospel so difficult and make it hard to live up to the standard. It has become a stumbling block to the next generation.

If we fail to present the gospel clearly, the next generation will suffer as so many have now. Statistics say that 70% of children that grew up in a Christian home will deny Christ by the time they are a sophomore in college. This is a travesty; it must be remedied. This cannot continue to happen, and this trend will be the demise of our Christian community. My passion for apologetics has led me to study intensely to better understand the Christian worldview. During the course of my study, I found that the Christian worldview is superior to any other worldview and it is logically sound.

I will share with you my journey into this world of evangelism and apologetics. You must understand, this is not going to be an intellectual debate discussing the philosophical theories or even a scholarly approach to what apologetics is all about; because I neither have the great intellectual capacity of doing so nor the deep thinking mind to be able to decipher like the great intellectual giants. I am simply a humble Bible-loving student seeking clarity of the Holy Scripture. However, I will give you my best when it comes to researching the necessary materials and reading all the relevant books, lectures, and dissertations from the intellectual giants of our day. The Bible will be the greatest source of truth for us to use in this apologetics book.

As you progress through this book, you will find that I have compiled enough information for you to be able to understand how to approach the Christian worldview. In my natural reading of the Bible, I was able to bring out the perspicuity of the Bible and show you the Christian Worldview. In turn, you can convey this to others in a meaningful and loving way. The Bible will be our core foundation of the Christian worldview.

1 Peter 3:15. But sanctify the Lord God in your hearts, and always be ready to give a defense to everyone who asks you a reason for the hope that is in you, with meekness and fear.

The Psalmist's lyrics tells us to taste and see that He is good and to take to heart the truth that God's word can abide in you for eternity. Consequently, Psalms 34:8 is my favorite scripture.

Psalm 34:8. Oh, taste and see that the Lord is good; Blessed is the man who trusts in Him!

The beautiful passage shows us that happiness comes to those who fear and trust the Lord; it ends with,

Psalms 34:10. The young lions lack and suffer hunger; But those who seek the Lord shall not lack any good thing.

Whenever I teach, my apologetic technique is to cleverly weave the student's lesson plan in such a way that the Christian worldview is presented. Before going on further, let's define the word "apologetics". It's not a descriptive word of being sorry for your action or excusing an offense; rather, it's an action word, meaning to defend a doctrine or theological discipline. Due to its emphasis on theology, which means study of God, our aspect of it mostly deals with religious issue. The Greek word "*apologia*" simply means "speaking in defense".

Apologetics should be part of your daily diet or vitamin supplement, taken every day to ensure spiritual healthiness. If you don't share what you know, you will not be replenished by the Holy Spirit. During my masters' study of apologetics, I realized that when the Holy Spirit reveals a new truth I have to share it. I am compelled to share my knowledge with you as the Holy Spirit reveals it to me. Similar to teaching science or math, I will employ the technique of explaining the Christian apologetics by understanding first the concept, then functionality, and then practical applications.

The world needs evangelism and believers to be able to defend the faith. We cannot take evangelism lightly because it is a matter of life and death—and even second death. If we fail to take account of the evangelistic nature of an argument, then we are doing a disservice to the people that we talk to. We cannot overlook the deepest need of the people that we talk to by not discerning why they ask the questions.

I believe that we need to approach the nature of apologetics from the biblical approach in our defense of faith. There is no such thing as a neutral position, because everyone has presupposition intent to their worldview. A question comes up; what is presupposition? It is something tacitly assumed beforehand at the beginning of a line of argument or course of action. In our case, what we know to be true starts with the Bible.

We are to be fully committed to the notion that the Bible is a book of history, science, literature, and philosophy. We cannot be led to think that being tolerant means we must put aside our source, the Bible. If we find ourselves deviating from a Christian commitment when it comes to defending the faith, then we are purposefully steering away from the only path of wisdom and truth found in the gospel of Jesus Christ. If we truly believe that the beginning of knowledge starts with our reverence of the Lord most high then we cannot be neutral in presenting our source of truth.

Proverbs 1:7. The fear of the Lord is the beginning of knowledge, but fools despise wisdom and instruction.

We are not to be drawn to use crafty speech or vain philosophy in presenting our Christian worldview. Our presupposition is to only be committed to Christ in the world of thought and firmly hang on to the teachings of the true Gospel. We must always bear in mind that salvation does not depend on our arguments or even winning the argument rather letting the Holy Spirit use our heartfelt words to bring a person to faith in Christ. In addition, we are to be gentle as we humbly and lovingly show the error of their ways, all the while praying that God may grant them repentance. A gentle reminder of this method is within this scripture:

1 Peter 3:15. But sanctify the Lord God in your hearts, and always be ready to give a defense to everyone who asks you a reason for the hope that is in you, with meekness and fear.

I have some good news and some bad news. Which do you want to hear first? Most people would say the bad news first please and then the good news. These idioms are used in our society as far back as the 1800s. As I begin to research the origin of the idiomatic phrase, it is very interesting to point out that people have used its formula to report news and even for delivering jokes. Here is a different example.

"Unless you point to the good news of God's grace people will not be able to bear the bad news of God's judgement," from *The Reason for God* by Timothy J. Keller.

Here is an example of a humorous anecdote involving some good news and some bad news. I feel a bit like the Indian chief that called the tribal council late one fall and said, "Listen, me got some good news and some bad news. First the bad news: the streams have all dried up, and all the game has gone north, and it is going to be a long cold winter, and we don't have any food, and all we have to eat is buffalo chips. Now the good news: we got 'em plenty buffalo chips."

Here's another one to chuckle to. Lewis and Clark were on an expedition. Lewis announced, "Men, I have some good news and some bad news. First the good news: we've covered more miles today than any other day on our entire trip, 50 miles. Now the bad news: we are lost."

Now how about if we explore some good news and some bad news from our church community.

Good news: The youth group used to come to the pastor's house on a surprise visit.

Bad news: Now they only come in the middle of the night, and they are armed with toilet paper and shaving cream to decorate the house.

Now, if you were a critical thinker, you would probably have seen the pattern in which the good news and bad news are being presented. I will give you a moment to think and ponder upon this, because after all, being an apologetic means that you are a thoughtful person. Have you noticed a pattern yet?

I am sure that many of you have noticed that when it comes to more serious matters most of us want you to present to us the bad news first, then the good news. However, when it comes to the matter of humor; it is often good timing and cleverness that is used when you present the good news first, followed by the bad news. The reason is that the bad news becomes the punchline. Have you ever wondered why this is so?

This concept was studied in an interesting paper by Angela Leg and Kate Sweeney in the March 2014 issue of *Personality and Social Psychology Bulletin*. In this study, participants filled out a personality inventory. One group was told that they were going to get feedback and that some of the feedback was going to be good and some bad. Which one did they want to hear first? A second group was told that they were going to give someone else feedback about their personality inventory. The feedback would contain some good news and bad news. They were asked what news they wanted to deliver first.

Most people, about 78%, wanted to hear the bad news first followed by the good news because they believe they would feel better if they got the bad news out of the way and ended on a good note. People delivering news were split. Those who imagined what a recipient would want to hear were likely to want to give the bad news first, while those who focused on their own feelings tended to want to give the good news first, because they felt it would be easier to start by giving good news.

Now that we have gotten the psychology of the good news and bad news concept, I will begin to lay out the structure of this book. In other words, this will be logically coherent as we deal with the subject of apologetics.

The Lord has put in my heart to share the gospel. Shortly after I accepted the Lord Jesus into my heart and confessed him before man that he is Lord of my life, in 1985, he revealed to me the meaning of Acts 9:15-16.

But the Lord said to him, "Go, for he is a chosen vessel of mine to bear My name before Gentiles kings and the children of Israel. For I will show him how many things he must suffer for My name's sake."

Of course, I did not know the full revelation of what this scripture meant until many years later. The heart of evangelism is within me with the gift of sharing the gospel of the Lord Jesus Christ, my Savior.

Before going further in revealing to you what this book is all about I would like for us to pray.

Heavenly father, thank you so much for revealing your awesome power and divine character to me and everyone that reads this book. You are a great God full of truth and power. I am sorry that, like many of my readers, I often take your grace for granted, and please forgive me for tolerating wickedness in my life. Also, forgive me for failing to tell others about your wrath against sin and your grace, thereby losing the true power of the gospel message.

May I never accept the fact that I am good enough for your salvation, but rather that I am a sinner who has found safety from your wrath as I cling to my Savior Jesus Christ who died for me over 2000 years ago and for all of my sins. Your grace renews every day so I may walk in the power of the Holy Spirit. Those who believe will say, amen.

"Evangelism" derives from the Greek word *evangelion* which means "good news". The gospel means good news. It's a message of how we can be saved from God's wrath. However, before we can receive the good news, we need to understand the bad news that God is intensely opposed to every manifestation of wickedness; He cannot tolerate sin in His presence. It is my intent to start with the bad news first. Without the bad news the good news is meaningless. Make no mistake; those who refuse to live by the truth should expect His full wrath and judgment. God has not hidden His character. It is evident in the created world and the inspired scriptures. One may not offer any excuse in the last day for not knowing that they are accountable to God. Only those without any wickedness by being forgiven will enter the kingdom of heaven.

Therefore, this is why we need to spread the gospel of God's message of grace, justice, and love that was portrayed on that cross over 2000 years ago. He rose three days later and now sits at the right hand of the throne of God. We need to know and others need to hear that Jesus is able to save us completely; this is the good news of the gospel. We must start by sanctifying our heart to align with the Lord God in order that we are ready to give a defense for answers to everyone who needs to know the reason that we have hope inside of our hearts, and we must also do this with so much care in the form of meekness and trembling of fear.

3

In this book we will know the truth. We will know how to detect what is truthful. We will also see the practical application of knowing what truth is. The truth lies within the Word of God.

I continued seeking the truth for years. It wasn't until I fully surrendered my sin-impaired-autonomous life and accepted fully the biblical worldview that I know I am on the right track. Along with that, I accepted all that the Christian worldview entails, like the effects of sin on human reasoning, my total reliance on God's power through his Holy Spirit and accepting my own natural inclination to always rebel against it. It was then that I was able to accept the truth of the Bible. If there is a doubt in your mind that my presupposition is that God exists and He has given us His Word, the Bible, that is the absolute truth. Now you may remove that doubt. I use the Bible as the basis for how to think, interpret evidence, explain the world around me, and to make sense of different parts of the books of the Bible.

I am not naïve to the fact that many of you have your own presupposition or a base for your beliefs. One's own presupposition has an effect on how they think, view the world, interpret evidence, and even read the Bible. In my experience, I have found that an atheist presupposition will most likely be that there is no God and that the truth is relative. An atheist believes that man decides what truth is; he interprets evidence and views the world and the morals within with that set of lenses.

In the process of evangelizing, we have to understand the questioners are more than the questions they ask. The mind and heart of the questioners is what we are after; the questions are the road that will take us to the questioners. God wants us to go after their heart and win them to the Kingdom of God. God is only interested in the heart; once He has it, He will get all of you.

As Christians we must always understand, realize, and believe that only the Holy Spirit can remove their unbelief. It is our job as Christian apologists to seek to uncover what these unbelievers' personal convictions are concerning the truth in all matters. Greg Koukl often says, "I just want to put a rock in your shoe". I get what he is saying. We want to ask just enough questions to make the conversation uncomfortable to their soul. We must help them uncover and move past their presupposition disbelief. We want to help them understand and answer life's basic questions. Questions such as, What is the nature of things? Which worldview makes the most sense? How does the world work? Where did it come from? What is man's place in the world? What is man's nature? What is morality? What's the proper method of knowing? How do I know what is real and what is not? In summary, answering the question about the origin, meaning, morality, and destiny of mankind.

Once we understand their general presupposition of their worldview, then we can compare that to the Christian worldview. I will show that the objections raised by unbelievers are answered within the biblical worldview. I will use the word of God in every argument because I know by doing this I am actually pitting the unbeliever against God and not my fallible thinking.

I want to share with all of you that I have an ache for the lost souls bound for destruction. This is my driving force behind this book. I will tackle every argument and offer reasons for our beliefs, but ultimately my spirit will be calling upon the Holy Spirit to do his work by using the soul-saving Gospel of Jesus Christ. This is how I know that I have successfully defended the faith that is in the Bible. The bottom line is salvation of the soul does not depend on our argument, but the Holy Spirit can use our sincere and authentic words to bring any person to faith in Christ. With the spirit of gentleness and humility, I will defend the faith and only lovingly correct their errors, all the while praying that God may grant them repentance.

4

The approach of telling you that I have some good news and some bad news is a biblical way of understanding the truth in the Word of God. After studying the Bible, I have concluded that God knows the outcome is the greatest fellowship between you and Him. He regrets that it has to start on a bad footing mainly caused by man. In other words, the Bible begins with telling you first the bad news, which is that His first creations have committed a grave sin. Rest assured I will end this book with the good news, which aligns with my goal of evangelism.

Realizing that this is a genre of humor that is often presented by comedians or humorists, I believe it makes this apologetics book easy to read. I wrote this book with my 10-year-old daughter in mind. I will lay out the apologetic terminologies, concepts, and philosophical questions in such a way that it is tangible to the average person. If you ever heard the saying "it's funny because it's true" then you will understand why I have chosen this approach of explaining the Christian worldview.

As you begin to read this book you will notice that I have intentionally laid it out in such a way that I am revealing the premise of the heart of the gospel. You will find that it follows the Bible starting with the book of Genesis. You will also find that as we explore each chapter, it is outlining the historical narrative of Genesis chapters one through eleven. I find that the best method to interpret the Word of God is through a historical grammatical approach. This ensures that the heart of the matter of the Word of God as it is being laid out in

Genesis is the truth. Many scholars of the New Testament utilize this method when interpreting the Old Testament. It is the only system that provides a series of checks and balances to keep us on track as we interpret it.

As we explore Genesis, we will carefully observe the text, context of each passage, and the clarity of the passages. We will also compare scriptures with other scriptures, the classification of the passages, and lastly the church's historical view. For those skeptics that challenge the inerrancy of the Word of God, I say this: God's Word has made the final and justifiable claim for itself that none of these other ancient texts have made. The Bible repeatedly asserts itself as the perfect Word of God. To the skeptics that want to discount the Old Testament, I say this to you: how we view the entire Scripture has great bearing on how we understand the gospel of Jesus Christ on which the whole Christian worldview is centered on. When we read the claims of the Scripture, we are left with no room for compromises. The Bible claims that all Scriptures come from God and not human will. The Bible also proclaims perfection in God and His Word, and any inconsistency or blemish is intolerable to biblical inerrancy and Gods infallibility. Who are you going to trust, the fallible man's interpretation or the claims of the infallible God?

I will proclaim Genesis one through eleven as straightforward, accurate, literal history because Jesus, the apostles, and all the other biblical writers did so. If Jesus accepts it as truth, that is good enough for me. There is absolutely no biblical basis for taking these chapters as any kind of non-literal, myth, or figurative genre of literature. The historical approach to Genesis one through eleven is the foundation for the Gospel and the future hope of mankind.

Let me be crystal clear; we achieve salvation when we repent of our sins and trust solely in the death and resurrection of Jesus Christ for our eternal life. However, if we trust in Christ and yet disbelieve Genesis, we are being inconsistent and not being faithful followers of our Lord. The most important thing to consider is that the proper interpretation of Genesis one through eleven is a question of the authority of God's Word.

We will enter the book of Genesis by understanding that the word Genesis is a Greek word that means "birth" or "beginnings". It is a proper title for the first book of the Bible. In a real sense, the book of Genesis serves as a prologue or an introduction to the rest of the Bible. Without Genesis, the Bible would be like a tree without roots.

1 Peter 2:6. Therefore it is also contained in the Scripture, "Behold, I lay in Zion a chief cornerstone, elect, precious, And he who believes on Him will by no means be put to shame."

That is exactly why we begin this book from the foundation. We know that a proper foundation is essential to having a strong fortress or a house. The central character in Genesis as in the Bible itself is God. It is certainly no accident that the book opens with the phrase "In the beginning God...". We must understand that God is the focus of this book we call the Bible. God does not have a need of anything; it is we that have every need for God. God exists! We need the word of God but the word of God does not need us to exist. The primary purpose of the book of Genesis is to teach us about God. Its teaching about creation, sin, judgment, election, and covenant all work together to explain this larger purpose.

As we explore the book of Genesis we will learn the character of God, which is that He is a great God, He is a demanding God, He is a loving God, He is a caring God. Genesis teaches us that God works through flawed human beings like you and me to achieve His purpose of grace. This is the essence of Christian apologetics. God through His Word created everything to glorify him.

Genesis is not the only book in the Bible that refers to God's creation of heaven and earth. Creation is the favorite theme in the Prophets, especially Isaiah 40:26, 28; 40:5; 43:1; 44:24; 45:5-7, 12, 18; 48:13; and Amos 4:13; 5:89; 9:56. The book of Job comes to its grand climax in chapters 38-42, and the theme of these chapters is also the creation. However, apart from Genesis, there is no book as rich in its celebration of creation of faith as the book of Psalms. In Psalms, creation is mentioned in 24:12; 95:36; 96: 45; 100:3; 136:39. It is the main focus of attention within Psalms 8:19:16; 29; 104; 148. These songs were written primarily to evoke a response of praise to the Creator from all his creatures. The praise theme is beautifully expressed in this Psalm:

Psalm 148:1. Praise the Lord! Praise the Lord from the heavens; Praise Him in the heights! 2. Praise Him, all His angels; Praise Him, all His hosts! 3. Praise Him, sun and moon; Praise Him, all you stars of light! 4. Praise Him, you heavens of heavens, And you waters above the heavens!

Then we will reveal the good news. We will explore the gospels. There are four gospels in the New Testament. Three of the gospels are the synoptic gospels; Matthew, Mark, and Luke. Those three gospels are synoptic because they view together the same story from slightly different perspectives. Though each has its own distinct voice and unique purpose, the three synoptic gospels are similar in the way they report the life of Christ. However, we will pay particular attention to John because he was called the beloved disciple. He was the only disciple that stayed by Jesus all the way to the cross. The gospel of John stands completely apart. Its style from a vantage point of Jesus' experience is radically different from the other three. John even tells us his purpose in writing his gospel in chapter 20:30-31.

John 20:30. And truly Jesus did many other signs in the presence of His disciples, which are not written in this book; 31. but these are written that you may believe that Jesus is the Christ, the Son of God, and that believing you may have life in His name.

Scholars have called this gospel the love gospel for a reason that is obvious. John, again, was the most loved of the disciples. John did not set out to write a complete history, but a select profile of his close friend Jesus. John tells us his purpose in writing the gospel is to provide a vital fulfilling life in the name of Jesus; the kind of life Jesus meant when he said, "I have come so they may have life and have it to the fullest." The gospel of John sounds more like a personal diary than a historical account and with good reason. It has such a personal flavor because it was written by the disciple of whom Jesus loved; John was the most intimate disciple of our Lord. During the days of his ministry, the tone of the writing reflects the bond of friendship between John and his Lord, Jesus. That is why this book has often been called the intimate gospel. This is precisely why I have chosen to study the good news according to John.

Father in heaven, may you reveal your holy goodness through this book. We pray that you will guide us and let us understand the scriptures within this book. In turn, we will use the knowledge to strengthen our faith and be equipped to give answers to those who ask. We ask this in the name of Jesus, amen.

ACKNOWLEDGMENTS

As an evangelical Christian, I believe the Bible is God's divine revelation. The Great Commission given to me by the Lord Jesus Christ is to make disciples of all nations. One can fulfill this great commission through the study of apologetics. We must stand firm in the inerrancy of the Word of God along with its practical application in our lives. The Word of God is the only source of truth; it is the foundation of the Christian worldview. The method and idea on how to teach and do apologetics should start with The Bible.

2 Timothy 3:16. All Scripture is given by inspiration of God, and is profitable for doctrine, for reproof, for correction, for instruction in righteousness.

The preservation of the authenticity, accuracy, and the apostolic nature of the Bible rests in the confidence that God breathed out His word into the minds of approximately 40 writers.

Proverbs 30:5. Every word of God is pure; He is a shield to those who put their trust in Him. 6. Do not add to His words, Lest He rebuke you, and you be found a liar.

Without the help of inspirational teachers and great men of God, my study on how to do apologetics would not be possible. John C. Whitcomb and Henry M. Morris wrote a great scientifically and historically accurate book called *The Genesis Flood.* It has helped me to dig deeper into understanding the scientific foundation of my apologetic research. Also, Ed Hindson and Ergun Caner's compilation of facts found within *The*

Popular Encyclopedia of Apologetics has helped me to survey the evidence for the truth of Christianity. I would like to give credit to Lee Strobel for writing *The Case for Christ* to inspire me to research the gospel of Jesus Christ. I have great respect and admiration for Dr. Frank Turek and Dr. Norman L. Geisler for producing such a great volume of research materials that have been like gold nuggets to me in my pursuit of how to do apologetics. The book *I Don't Have Enough Faith to Be an Atheist* has changed my perspective and increased my knowledge of the Bible ten-fold. Gregory Koukl has written a most useful and practical book called *Tactics*. It has given me clever skills to defend the faith with meekness and trembling. Francis Chan, since his appearance with Ravi Zacharias during the Church Leader Conference on May 23, 2019, has provoked me to make the Holy Spirit a real part of my ministry. The book *The Forgotten God* is refreshing and thought provokingly relevant in my daily walk of salvation. The book *Seven Mile Miracle* by Steven Furtick inspired me to preach again after twenty years of slumber. Jentezen Franklin's book *Love like You've Never Been Hurt* did exactly what it intended to do. Ken Ham's books *The Lie: Evolution* and *Six Days or Millions of Years* were instrumental in shaping my mind to the truth of history of the world. I sincerely want to thank these great men of God for their contribution to the Kingdom of Heaven within my life. I have also been inspired tremendously through the reading of Dr. Jason Lisle's *The Ultimate Proof of Creation: Resolving the Origins Debate*.

I want to thank everyone within the Institute for Creation Research for their generous support to enable me to have the knowledge to write this book. Ken Ham and the Answers in Genesis team have been instrumental in shaping my thoughts and understanding that science can only be true because of the Bible.

My heartfelt thank you would not be totally complete without dedicating a column to the elite set of God's Prophets for the modern times that have helped build what we know as the "29th Chapter of Acts" Church. Without these intellectual giants, people like me would have very little chance to be knowledgeable enough to do an apologetic ministry. I pray for the Lord to give them a special place in the new Heavens and the new Earth for their contribution to our time. These men and their books include Cornelius Van Til, Greg Bahnsen's *Van Til's Apologetics* and *Always Ready*, and Ken Ham and associates' "Answers in Genesis" articles.

They have made it possible for me to follow the apostle Peter's apologetic prescription to sanctify the Lord God within my life, always being prepared to make a defense to any questioners who asked me why I have the great hope and true joy, while doing it with gentleness and respect, even when I am slandered, so those who revile my good message in Christ may be put to shame but their soul might be saved (1 Peter 3:15).

CHAPTER 1
THE BEGINNING OF THE UNIVERSE

Dr. VanDoom: Your tests show you have only 24 hours to live.

Elder McVicker: Ouch! What's the good news?

Dr. VanDoom: That was the good news.

Elder McVicker: Ouch again, so what is the bad news?

Dr. VanDoom: I forgot to call you yesterday!

If there had been newspapers in the beginning of time, one of them if not all might have carried this headline: "Creator Creates Creation." This is what Genesis 1:1-5 is all about. God the Creator created the entire universe in a time-frame of six days followed by a seventh day of rest. God rested, but not because He was tired. It reflects a pause or completed task. This is discussed further within the next chapter. The Scriptures read like this:

Genesis 1:1. In the beginning God created the heavens and the earth. 2. The earth was without form, and void; and darkness was on the face of the deep. And the Spirit of God was hovering over the face of the waters.

3. Then God said, "Let there be light"; and there was light. 4. And God saw the light, that it was good; and God divided the light from the darkness. 5. God called the light Day, and the darkness He called Night. So the evening and the morning were the first day.

It is profoundly clear to me that these passages marked the first day of creation. How does this fare with the idea of the big bang? The big bang is a story that derives from secular science. Does Genesis 1:1 state that the big bang story is wrong or untrue?

First, let's define it. The big bang is a story that suggests that billions of years ago the universe began in a tiny, infinitely hot and dense point called singularity. This singularity containing mass and energy exploded to create not only space but everything that is in the universe. Although this is the simple version of it, it is what is being taught as truth in science class. I know because I have seen it in textbooks.

The big bang has many scientific flaws, and it forces one to accept blind faith. One could research a number of scientific theories that disprove this: The Flatness Problem, Inflating the Complexities, Baryon number problem, Missing Population III Stars, and others. The Bible-believing Christian understands that the big bang is false because it is contrary to what the Bible says about the origin of the universe. There are many case scenarios, papers, and a cosmological principle conundrum that have disproved the big bang model. It is very encouraging to see many scientific studies that have demonstrated problems and undermining assumptions fundamental to the big bang story.

Although Genesis was written with a slightly different purpose in mind, it does give evidence into the origin of the universe from a scientific investigation point of view. The big bang erroneously assumes that the universe came from nothing, which violates the law of biogenesis. Biogenesis states that matter can't come from non-matter or life from non-life. However, the best argument against it is to point out that it goes against the authority of the Word of God. The straightforward reading and plain meaning of the Scripture is that God created the universe.

Genesis 1:1. In the beginning God created the heavens and the earth.

We will approach the scripture in this manner to understand it fully. We will carefully observe the text, context of each passage, the clarity of the passages, comparing scriptures with other scriptures, the classification of the passages, and lastly the churches' historical view. We will understand the meaning by reading what it says, not what outside sources say.

During a Bible study session, Lily asked what seemed like two innocent questions from a young and eager mind of a 10-year-old. But as I began to contemplate the answer, I realized that there was a depth there that some scholars are using as a current philosophical study. The questions were phrased like this: "What does the Bible mean by face of the deep? Why was God hovering over the face of the waters and not looking from the outside of his creation?"

This alludes to the many theories that are presented to the world from some Christian scholars. What comes to my mind is the Gap Theory, a long gap time between Genesis 1:1-2, suggesting a world that existed within and destroyed.

God created the universe in six days as described in Genesis. The theory falls flat before it could get any wind to help lift it up. This idea has been debunked as lacking biblical support because it suggests that death came before sin and not what the Scripture says, death as the consequence of sin. This compromise, perhaps to accommodate a millions-of-years theory, fails miserably because it simply isn't in the Scripture.

Skeptics argue that the Hebrew grammar of Genesis 1:1-2 makes it possible, but this is an unnatural interpretation; the plain meaning of straight reading of the text doesn't support it. One could go on by explaining the grammarian Gesenius' long explanation of contextual meaning, but I will not. If you are looking for that depth of knowledge, my book will be found wanting. This writer intends to keep the argument simple enough for an average person to understand.

Let's get back to the 2nd question: why was the Spirit of God hovering over the face of the waters and not looking from the outside of His creation? Lily seems to understand that God the Creator has to be outside time, matter, and space. She explained to me succinctly by saying one can't create a computer game and be in the game itself. I think Dr. Turek and Dr. Geisler would be proud to know that their concept is attainable by a 10-year-old mind such as hers.

The Spirit of God is breaking through the void and darkness to show the need for light to separate it. Then God separated the void by creating light. The word "deep" in this passage is an implication of primeval waters that merely stretch endlessly from pole to pole. It probably covered all the earth. This suggests chaos in the form of water described as without form and void. Looking in-depth, the word for "without form" in Hebrew is *tofu*. This means desert waste. In addition, the word void in Hebrew is *vohu.* It is used in Jeremiah 4:23 and normally follows the word *tōhoku* which in essence it strengthens its meaning.

Jeremiah 4:23. I beheld the earth, and indeed it was without form, and void; And the heavens, they had no light.

So these two words show chaos and state of waste. Make no mistake, the darkness that is covering the face of this chaotic water is understood as total darkness. This makes the creation of life prominent, and it supports the idea that light is created. This natural reading results in a straight interpretation of the Scripture; some might refer to this as "exegesis". Exegesis is critical explanation or interpretation of a text, especially of scriptures. It doesn't require any outside thinking or advice to interpret the Scripture, unlike eisegesis. Eisegesis is to import a subjective, preconceived idea into the meaning of the text.

However, it seems that a growing number of scholars that are trying to re-interpret the beginning of the universe by suggesting that it cannot be a literal translation. As one views the debate of Hugh Ross and Walter Kaiser against Ken Ham and Jason Lyle about the old earth and young earth, the conclusion was the literal translation of Genesis is the most logical and sound. You may judge for yourself by watching the debate on YouTube dated November 21, 2016. The traditional understanding of Genesis 1:1 is trustworthy and sound. In the beginning God did indeed create the heavens and the earth out of nothing; God spoke it into existence.

As one reads this passage, it reveals how our heart is being represented by the total darkness of the universe and when the light of the Holy Spirit visits us and occupies our heart that is when the darkness can be driven out. As Paul writes in this Scripture, we learn what that light means.

2 Corinthians 4:6. For it is the God who commanded light to shine out of darkness, who has shone in our hearts to give the light of the knowledge of the glory of God in the face of Jesus Christ.

Paul considers this scripture as historical, factual, and a plainly understood text. It points to a real event in history, the creation of light around 6000 years ago as recorded in Genesis. God revealed to Paul that it is more than just a recorded history. God showed us through Paul that His acts in creation would be like cosmic words, foretelling spiritual things to come. To those who are in Christ, the light will be revealed.

John 1:7. This man came for a witness, to bear witness of the Light, that all through him might believe.

Jesus is the Light that breaks apart the darkness that is in the world.

Another question asked: what is a scholar? A scholar is a person who is knowledgeable in a particular field of study. However, some scholars will bring their worldview into their study, using their theories to fit into the Bible what isn't there. This is called presupposition.

Genesis is the book of beginnings. It recounts the beginning of everything — everything, that is, except for God. Most apologetic teachers will warn you about the impending question, which would be, "Who created God?" One of the best answers that would show our meekness towards them would be that the God of the Bible, my God, has to be apart from His creation. In other words, God has to be spaceless, timeless, and immaterial. The Bible makes no effort either to define or to defend His existence.

Hebrews 6:13. For when God made a promise to Abraham, because He could swear by no one greater, He swore by Himself.

It merely assumes that He is the uncreated Creator, that he existed before creation began, that he is not identified with it and that he is in no way dependent upon it.

Genesis 1:1, "In the beginning God created the heavens and the earth," is usually interpreted as the title and not as the chain of events of creation, which is found in Genesis 1:12-13. In other words, it provides a summary of everything that is taking place step-by-step in the verses that follow. Here, it is stated that God created the heavens and the earth. The Hebrew verb *bara* which means "to create" occurs 40 times in the Old Testament and always has God as its subject. Creation is never spoken of as a human activity. It is always an activity of God; for this reason, some Bible scholars have interpreted the verb to mean "to create out of nothing". While it is true that God created out of nothing, the verb itself does not necessarily convey this meaning. It states that God created everything that was created. It is worth noting again that God spoke into existence the entirety of all things that He created.

John 1:1. In the beginning was the Word, and the Word was with God, and the Word was God. 2. He was in the beginning with God. 3. All things were made through Him, and without Him nothing was made that were made.

God uses His Word to bring everything into existence.

Next follows in a very orderly account of creation Genesis 1:12-13.

Genesis 1:12. And the earth brought forth grass, the herb that yields seed according to its kind, and the tree that yields fruit, whose seed is in itself according to its kind. And God saw that it was good. 13. So the evening and the morning were the third day.

The inanimate world of things took shape on the first four days. Lily asked, "What is inanimate?" The answer is simply not alive or non-living. This included light, the firmament, dry land, seas, plants, sun, moon, and stars. To those who worship these inanimate objects, God does not permit it in the Bible.

It is perceived that Lily's question goes beyond the simple meaning of living beings. Many of the science textbooks point out the biological condition of being alive as being able to ingest food and grow. They don't just elude but demand that plants are living creatures. However, the Bible makes a clear distinction between human and animals as having life or a living soul contrary to plants which have no living soul. The Bible uses the Hebrew term *nephesh chayyâh* which means "living soul" or "creature with soul" when referring to humankind and animal. It never applies to plant life. This is within the context in Genesis 1:20-30.

God created all plant kinds on day three as listed in Genesis 1:11.

Genesis 1:11. Then God said, "Let the earth bring forth grass, the herb that yields seed, and the fruit tree that yields fruit according to its kind, whose seed is in itself, on the earth"; and it was so.

Plants were made as a source of food for Adam and Eve. It wasn't until after the flood that God allowed Noah to eat animals.

With that explanation arrives another question about God's light; what is it? What comes to one's mind may be to explain the evidentiary proof of what Isaac Newton discovered around 1600. He used a prism, shining a white light into it to cause seven different colors to come out of it. It is one's understanding that when light slowed down, the seven visible colors appeared to the naked eyes. This evidentiary proof through observable science caused Lily to have a perplexed look. She exclaimed, "So God is a bright white light and can turn to color if it is slowed down?" Of course, this warrants additional explanations. This writer began to dig through the Bible and came across this.

2 Corinthians 4:6. For it is the God who commanded light to shine out of darkness, who has shone in our hearts to give the light of the knowledge of the glory of God in the face of Jesus Christ.

Paul uses this historically accurate account to make a spiritual connection with the people. His writing was to prove that God was showing us that a cosmic event proves a foretelling of spiritual things to come. God's phrase "let there be light" is a message to the broken, helpless, and sinful people that "Christ in you is the restorative hope." As the world was dark and void, so is our existence without God. God's grace is translated into "let there be light."

John 1:4. In Him was life, and the life was the light of men. 5. And the light shines in the darkness, and the darkness did not comprehend it.

Later within the same chapter verse 9 states "that was the true Light which gives light to every man coming into the world." Like Paul, John used the same idea in Genesis 1:3 to point out God's intended plan to use the true account of light creation to show a greater spiritual awakening within our minds. Only God can make you righteous. We can use the same thought process of Paul and John by using a true historical account to point us to God's miraculous power of light to make us righteous.

Let us pray that the life-changing power of the Holy Spirit speaks to our mind about our sinful nature and our willful disobedience of God almighty. May He, who is able to search the depths of our hearts, bring you to repentance and accept the redemption power of the cross. We can agree that we are sinners in need of saving. Please, Lord Jesus, come into our hearts because we believe that you have died on the cross for us. As we rise to accept your forgiveness, we must believe that God has raised Jesus from the dead, and through the power of the Holy Spirit, we will walk with you in faith and help you build your kingdom on earth as it is in heaven. All those who believe will say, amen.

As we continue digging into the creation process, the animate world (consisting of sea creatures, birds, land animals, and humans) was created on the fifth and sixth days of the creation week. Each of these phases of creation ended in conferring of authority.

Genesis 1:16. Then God made two great lights: the greater light to rule the day, and the lesser light to rule the night. He made the stars also.

On the sixth day, He gave men and women dominion over all other living creatures that he had made.

Genesis 1:28. Then God blessed them, and God said to them, "Be fruitful and multiply; fill the earth and subdue it; have dominion over the fish of the sea, over the birds of the air, and over every living thing that moves on the earth."

A question arises about the meaning of the word "dominion". Christians are often accused of being uncaring about the world around us. On the contrary, God has given us the responsibility of having sovereignty or control of the world; this is what the word dominion is referring to. What does that look like in practical application? It requires more than just observing from the distance; it requires personal involvement. Like a parent to a child, God wants us to care about His creations, especially the animals.

God even tasked Adam to name the animals. This would give Adam a bond like that of a father and a child. Skeptics use this as a criticism of the Bible. They claim that this task is too cumbersome for Adam, when the reality is God only instructed him to name land animals, and he did do it within 24 hours prior to Eve's creation. This is possible because the Bible says Adam named only kinds of land animals, which includes the cattle, birds of the air, and beast of the fields. That's not very much, and Adam had a perfect brain because he was a perfect man. So, this is entirely true and possible.

While God would care for His creation with unseen power, He instructs us to care with a more direct and hands-on approach. God asks us to subdue the earth in a more visible way.

Genesis 1:28. Then God blessed them, and God said to them, "Be fruitful and multiply; fill the earth and subdue it; have dominion over the fish of the sea, over the birds of the air, and over every living thing that moves on the earth."

God equipped us with intelligence and language in order to care, rule, and judge all that He created. Our job as humans is to study and understand the world so we can judge wisely and care deeply. We are accountable to God on how well we care, manage, and judge the world that He has bestowed upon us. We will be held accountable on how well we do as overseers of His creation. In short, true Christians are the greatest earth lovers and environmentalists because we are accountable to a higher authority which is the Word of God.

Genesis 1:26. Then God said, "Let Us make man in Our image, according to Our likeness; let them have dominion over the fish of the sea, over the birds of the air, and over the cattle, over all the earth and over every creeping thing that creeps on the earth." 27. So God created man in His own image; in the image of God He created him; male and female He created them. 28. Then God blessed them, and God said to them, "Be fruitful and multiply; fill the earth and subdue it; have dominion over the fish of the sea, over the birds of the air, and over every living thing that moves on the earth."

Verse 27 refers to the creation of male and female—sex—and later in Genesis chapter two, we read the creation of man and woman—gender—in more detail. Moreover, God of the Bible confirms the study of genetics that points to the X and Y chromosomes which determine the sex of a human. Females have XX chromosomes and males have XY chromosomes. The sex region of the Y chromosome, SRY, is a gene that inhibits female anatomical growth and induces the formation of male anatomy about 6 to 8 weeks after fertilization in the womb.

Although most of us are aware of our anatomical differences, there are also many physiological differences as well to be noted. The Bible is in agreement with the science of biology about gender and sex. God created male man, named Adam, and female woman, named Eve. It is important to point out that at the end of this chapter God saw everything that he had made and indeed it was very good. We do not underestimate the importance of the two simple words "very good"; it supports the idea that everything that was created and placed in the garden of Eden was flawless and had a nature of goodness.

It is clear to me that there was no sickness, disease, nor death. Some secular scientists and even some Christians would try to insert the idea of millions or billions of years of evolution. Fossil records have concluded that some animals died before man's creation that had diseases such as cancer. However, this undermines the authority of the Word of God. God created everything and it was very good, that means perfect in every form and condition.

Heavenly Father, thank you for speaking to our hearts that everything was created perfectly, in every sense of the words "very good". We pray that the Holy Spirit reveals the knowledge explained above into our hearts and minds. We pray for understanding and perspicuity of the scripture. We ask this in the powerful name of Jesus, amen.

CHAPTER 2
THE BEGINNING OF LIFE

Church secretary: I am praying for you, pastor, and I have some good news and some bad news.

Chuck Olsen: Thank you! What is the good news?

Church secretary: The Women's Guild voted to send you a get-well card.

Chuck Olsen: That is good news, so is there a bad news?

Church secretary: The vote passed by 31-30.

Beginning in chapter two of Genesis, God gave an account that He was finished by using the affirmation words "very good"; it showed that He was satisfied with what he had done. God is proud of his creation and it was shown even in the earliest book of the Bible by subject matter. (We know that Job was the earliest written book.)

Job 38:7. ...when the morning stars sang together, and all the sons of God shouted for joy?

It is important to note that God is boasting about his creation by stating that it is very good. When God created humankind, He fulfilled every purpose which He had designed. This speaks volumes to my heart. God says to me that He sees his creation as very good and that includes us.

Genesis 2:1. Thus the heavens and the earth, and all the host of them, were finished. 2. And on the seventh day God ended His work which He had done, and He rested on the seventh day from all His work which He had done.

Genesis 1:31. Then God saw everything that He had made, and indeed it was very good. So the evening and the morning were the sixth day.

This brings up a question from the 10-year-old. What does "God rested" mean? Can God really be tired? We briefly touched on this question in the last chapter. He can't be tired because He is omnipotent, which is having unlimited power. This doesn't suggest that He needs a day off or anything like that.

Isaiah 40:28. Have you not known? Have you not heard? The everlasting God, the Lord, the Creator of the ends of the earth, neither faints nor is weary. His understanding is unsearchable.

This scripture solidifies the idea that God was not necessarily exhausted, which would mean that He has to rest. Rather, it is the ceasing of the labor of creation. It's a command that He later reiterates in the commandment given to Moses that we should pause from labor of every kind. God rested because He had accomplished His work. God "rested" in Hebrew is *shabat* translated as "seventh"; also from another Hebrew word *saba*. The word *saba* means complete. In essence, God had completed his creation. Some have explained its relation to the Sabbath, as we will come across later in Exodus.

But if you look closely, God did not instruct Adam to rest on the seventh day or make any reference yet to the Sabbath. Bible scholars are not exactly sure why, except for the notion He was saving this command for Israel as part of an external sign of the covenant God made with the Jews. This would happen later, in Exodus 16:23. God reminded the children of Israel of what He did during creation, as He gave them the Sabbath as a day of rest. This is a gift for man, not man for it.

Mark 2:27. And He said to them, "The Sabbath was made for man, and not man for the Sabbath. 28. Therefore the Son of Man is also Lord of the Sabbath."

God has created our body to work for six days and rest on the seventh. The gift of replenishment is confirmed by the science of biology; our body needs to rebuild and regenerate. There's a Latin term that describes this; it is *imago Dei*, which is "image of God". It is a symbiotic relationship between God and humanity; it makes perfect sense that we do what God does when it comes to work and rest. God's instruction to us is clear on the need to pause or take a break from our normal activity in order to worship. It is His divine purpose for us to live our lives to the fullest but never forsake the pausing to worship God.

God is simply trying to teach us a recreate-to-blessing power that we could get by recognizing a pause moment within a seven-day work week to worship and give God the glory and the honor. God gave us the ability to be productive and the power to reproduce. This happens best only when we pause to worship Him in spirit and truth. By recognizing the Sabbath as a day of rest, we can stimulate, enrich, and restore fullness to our spirit, mind, and soul. This is the heart of *imago Dei*.

A question arises from the young mind in regard to soul and spirit. What is the difference between soul and spirit? In Genesis 2:7, the spirit is referred to as the meaning of "breath of Life".

Genesis 2:7. And the Lord God formed man of the dust of the ground, and breathed into his nostrils the breath of life; and man became a living being.

How this is different from the soul, the Bible doesn't make too much of a distinction. In fact, the words "soul" and "spirit" are interchangeable. James 2:26 makes an assertion that without the spirit the body is dead in speaking about faith, so without the works faith is also dead.

James 2:26. For as the body without the spirit is dead, so faith without works is dead also.

Whereas in 1 Corinthians 7:34, Christians were instructed to be holy in body and spirit, similarly in 1 Peter 1:22 we are to purify our souls by obeying the truth.

1 Corinthians 7:34. There is a difference between a wife and a virgin. The unmarried woman cares about the things of the Lord, that she may be holy both in body and in spirit. But she who is married cares about the things of the world—how she may please her husband.

1 Peter 1:22. Since you have purified your souls in obeying the truth through the Spirit in sincere love of the brethren, love one another fervently with a pure heart.

It is interesting to note that when David rejoices or sings praise, he uses the word "soul" in Psalm 103:1;

"Bless the Lord, O my soul…" But with the Apostle Paul, in 1 Corinthians 14:14-15, he is praying in a tongue, his spirit prays and he continues to pray in spirit.

Psalms 103:1. Bless the Lord, O my soul; And all that is within me, bless His holy name!

1 Corinthians 14:14. For if I pray in a tongue, my spirit prays, but my understanding is unfruitful. 15. What is the conclusion then? I will pray with the spirit, and I will also pray with the understanding. I will sing with the spirit, and I will also sing with the understanding.

If we dig deeper into the Hebrew word for each, it is *nephesh* for soul and *ruach* for spirit. The word *nephesh* is used twice as many times as the word *ruach.* This is probably because *nephesh* can be used to describe not only humans but animals. It leads me to believe that there's a slight distinction between soul and spirit. *Ruach* never refers to animal beings. We also need to know that when *ruach* is used to describe God, it never means biological living beings rather an immaterial being, a seat of mind.

When used to refer to human beings, it is mostly holistic unity of soul and body with a great emphasis on functionality. The spirit takes on a meaning of an entity that consists of will, mind, emotion, and a moral disposition. We can see these references within Psalms 51:12, Isaiah 29:24, and Proverbs 18:14.

Psalms 51:12. Restore to me the joy of Your salvation, And uphold me by Your generous Spirit.

Isaiah 29:24. These also who erred in spirit will come to understanding, And those who complained will learn doctrine."

Proverbs 18:14. The spirit of a man will sustain him in sickness, But who can bear a broken spirit?

Although humans and animals have a similar *nephesh*, the Bible states that humans were created in the image of God to rule over the animals. The *ruach* within us gives us the ability to store knowledge, to perceive, to form beliefs and desires, and to evaluate choices and actions to decide a favorable or unfavorable outcome. Animals lack these things; they are not equal to man.

Ecclesiastes 3:21. Who knows the spirit of the sons of men, which goes upward, and the spirit of the animal, which goes down to the earth?

This suggests that animals' spirits do not ascend, which I would assume refers to heaven.

1 Corinthians 2:11. For what man knows the things of a man except the spirit of the man which is in him? Even so no one knows the things of God except the Spirit of God.

God has created our spirit to connect to God's spirit. But is it that simple? The answer is a little more complicated than just that. Let's dig deeper.

The thought that the Bible is referring to as man's mental state is belief, sensation, feeling, and desire. The person's mental state lies within his consciousness. Therefore when he lacks the spirit, he will not know what he believes, sensations he feels, or desires. When we connect our spirit—which is our will, desires, and beliefs—to God's Spirit—His will, desires, and intent—then we can achieve oneness with Him. That is the mystery that's been revealed.

Colossians 1:26. ...the mystery which has been hidden from ages and from generations, but now has been revealed to His saints. 27. To them God willed to make known what are the riches of the glory of this mystery among the Gentiles: which is Christ in you, the hope of glory.

For the sake of clarity, we can know our own mental awareness through our desires, beliefs, and sensations. God's thoughts are known to us by the same awareness.

Next, God explained how His garden was kept lush and green because every creature needed it for food. God used water vapor to appear from along the edge of the atmosphere. Consequently, this vapor mist was present at the end of creation day two in Genesis 1:6-8.

Genesis 1:6. Then God said, "Let there be a firmament in the midst of the waters, and let it divide the waters from the waters." 7. Thus God made the firmament, and divided the waters which were under the firmament from the waters which were above the firmament; and it was so. 8. And God called the firmament Heaven. So the evening and the morning were the second day.

The plentiful mist indicates that the earth never would need rain, which explains why Noah's message was difficult to believe by the people of his day. Scholars believe that rain did not start falling from the sky until God caused the canopy to break, bringing down torrential rain during the great global flood. This speaks truth to me because the creation story follows the coherent path that seems to explain other parts of the book. After God prepared the earth for habitation, He created his masterpiece. God formed humankind; He created man called Adam.

Genesis 2:7. And the Lord God formed man of the dust of the ground, and breathed into his nostrils the breath of life; and man became a living being.

It describes the forming of the human body from dust of the ground, which explained why the Hebrew word *adamah* is used. The word formed comes from the Hebrew word *yassar*, which means “to mold”. Scholars suggest that the same word usually refers to when an artist creates a beautiful masterpiece. We are God’s masterpiece and we are fashioned from the dust of the earth.

This explains why most of the mass of the human body is made up of six elements: carbon, oxygen, hydrogen, nitrogen, calcium, and phosphorous. All of these elements are found on earth. We are God’s crowning achievement because He has designed us with care as a master sculptor would.

Again, He also added breath of life, with the Hebrew term *ruach* being used in the Old Testament also as spirit. We are the only being that was created by God with soul, spirit, and body. Unlike animals, God imbued humankind with spirit that not only can fellowship with Him but also can live eternally. This is why we are created in the image of God.

Do our physiological and physical similarities make us the same as animals? Secular scientists have inferred that we are human animals. The simple fact is this: God formed man from the dust of the ground, and the Lord God had also formed out of the ground all the beasts of the fields. However, that is the only similarity. Man is formed in the image of God and animals were not. Man has body, mind, and spirit. On the other hand, animals only have body and soul. Animals can't worship or acknowledge God's presence. In Genesis 2:19 animals are described as living creatures, whereas man is described as a living being in Genesis 2:7.

Genesis 2:19. Out of the ground the Lord God formed every beast of the field and every bird of the air, and brought them to Adam to see what he would call them. And whatever Adam called each ***living creature,*** *that was its name.*

Genesis 2:7. And the Lord God formed man of the dust of the ground, and breathed into his nostrils the breath of life; and man became a ***living being***.

On further study into the Hebrew word *nephesh* which can mean breath, we can confirm that it was being used for both animals and man. I would like to point out that the effects of the flood were told in Genesis 7:22.

Genesis 7:22. All in whose nostrils was the breath of the spirit of life, all that was on the dry land, died.

Every living thing was wiped out, including the creatures that move along the ground and the birds of the air.

Another look into the word *nephesh* in Genesis 9:4 explains that life is in the blood.

Genesis 9:4. But you shall not eat flesh with its life, that is, its blood.

The bottom line is God regards man differently from animals. The Bible account is primarily concerned with the relationship between God and man. Man was created by God in His image. Although the earth was created for animals to have a place within God's world, He has given man dominion over the animals.

Romans 8:19. For the earnest expectation of the creation eagerly waits for the revealing of the sons of God. 20. For the creation was subjected to futility, not willingly, but because of Him who subjected it in hope; 21. because the creation itself also will be delivered from the bondage of corruption into the glorious liberty of the children of God.

Adam was created from the earth by God; he was given a helper created from his rib, his wife Eve. The Bible has been confirmed by science that the substance of his flesh, sinews, and bones consists of the very same elements as the soil which forms the crust of the earth and the limestone that lies embedded in its bowels. Adam and Eve are the first humankind made from the materials that are in the earth. A celebration of this is reflected within Psalms 139:14.

Psalms 139:14. I will praise you, for I am fearfully and wonderfully made; marvelous are your works; and that my soul knows very well.

The Garden of Eden, which means "pleasure, delight" in Hebrew (and the Greek word is *paradeisos* which means "enclosed park"), is located in the east. It is not southern Mesopotamia where Eden geographically is located, despite many hypotheses regarding the location of the rivers. Let's take a closer look inside the garden, starting with verse nine.

Genesis 2:9. And out of the ground the Lord God made every tree grow that is pleasant to the sight and good for food. The tree of life was also in the midst of the garden, and the tree of the knowledge of good and evil. 10. Now a river went out of Eden to water the garden, and from there it parted and became four riverheads.

The tree of life provided Adam with eternal sustenance. The tree of knowledge of good and evil serves two purposes for Adam. First, the tree serves as a reminder that God seeks obedience from Adam. Second, the tree signifies the free will to love and serve God willingly or to rebel against Him.

This is perfect love; perfect love embodies God's personality and His essence. Love untested cannot be perfect love. God is personifying to mankind and teaching Adam about the true nature of love. He will show His sacrificial love through His son Jesus for the atonement of Adam's sin later on.

This satisfies as an answer for why God put a temptation in a form of the tree of knowledge of good and evil; a social experiment argument. It would be ludicrous to suggest that the tree is evil in any way, because that would contradict Genesis 1:31.

Genesis 1:31. Then God saw everything that He had made, and indeed it was very good. So the evening and the morning were the sixth day.

We can assess that the tree of knowledge of good and evil serves as an opportunity for man to obey or disobey God, but the wickedness does not lie within the tree. Man's disobedience lies within Adam and Eve when they choose to disobey God's command.

Although the Scripture states that God was Adam's constant companion and provider, Adam was missing something. Despite all the luxurious amenities that the garden provided, there was no human companionship for Adam. He was alone.

He was so lonely that God became aware of it and decided to do something about it in Genesis 2:18. God saw that despite the many creatures created from the same ground that He created Adam from, none of them suited to be his companion.

Genesis 2:18. And the Lord God said, "It is not good that man should be alone; I will make him a helper comparable to him."

God decided that a helper was needed that would be suited for the man. Suitability means that this companion would fulfill not only the physical and the mental need, but also a spiritual union for them to be content with each other. Verse 23 confirms this union when Adam said, "This is now bone of my bones and flesh of my flesh; she shall be called Woman because she was taken out of Man."

Verse 24: "Therefore a man shall leave his father and mother and be joined to his wife and they shall become one flesh." This is marriage defined as God would intend mankind to have. Adam's outburst of joy constitutes the first human speech recorded in the Bible. This perfect union between the first man and the first woman recorded in the Bible signifies God's plan for a community and fellowship. The touching emotional cry of discovery within verse 23, expressed in a poetic form, is refreshing and joyful.

While Adam slept he had been relieved of one of his ribs; therefore when he saw the woman he blurted out “flesh of my flesh”. The woman, Eve, signifies completeness. The perfect truth in this verse is this: in a marriage, a man and a woman complete each other. This perfect union is the ability for two beings to achieve a quality of life through a bonding of soul and body. With the invention of marriage, creation reaches its goal in a mutual and complementary society that we now know as family. Man and woman were created for relationship, and the highest expression of human relationship is in the holy matrimony, what we call marriage.

Ecclesiastes 4:9. Two are better than one, because they have a good reward for their labor. 10. For if they fall, one will lift up his companion. But woe to him who is alone when he falls, for he has no one to help him up. 11. Again, if two lie down together, they will keep warm; but how can one be warm alone? 12. Though one may be overpowered by another, two can withstand him. And a threefold cord is not quickly broken.

The Scriptures tells us that two is better than one, because they have a good reward for their labor. A marriage between a man and a woman with God is like a threefold cord and is not quickly broken. Ephesians 5:22-33 confirms the goodness of marriage. It points out how a husband should love his wife as Christ loves the church.

The concept of marriage comes from the Word of God. It is a union between man and woman, and it is sacred. God will only bless the union when it is practiced in its proper context and form.

Heavenly Father, we thank you for giving us the depth of understanding on how you have created our universe and everything in it. We pray that this knowledge will strengthen our faith in you and your greatness within our lives. We give you the glory and the honor forever, in Jesus' name we pray, amen.

CHAPTER 3
THE BEGINNING OF SIN AND CURSE

Church secretary: I have some good news and some bad news, pastor.

Villard Hunter: Give me the good news first.

Church secretary: Church attendance rose dramatically the last three weeks.

Villard Hunter: Wow! That is good news. So what's the bad news?

Church secretary: Too bad you were on vacation.

Up to this moment within the Bible, we are told by God seven times that it, creation, was good. But we know that things are about to take a bad turn; they were not going to live happily ever after in the Garden of Eden. The couple was about to encounter something that would counter their innocence; that is, the possibility of defying their Creator. It is known that one of the greatest apologetics in recent times was a man named Clive Staples Lewis. He is known most for creating the world of Narnia.

In *The Case for Christianity*, C. S. Lewis writes the following.

"God created things which had free will. That means creatures which can go wrong or right. Some people think they can imagine a creature which was free but had no possibility of going wrong, but I can't. If a thing is free to be good it's also free to be bad. And free will is what has made evil possible. Why, then, did God give them free will? Because free will, though it makes evil possible, is also the only thing that makes possible any love or goodness or joy worth having. A world of automata—of creatures that worked like machines—would hardly be worth creating. The happiness which God designs for His higher creatures is the happiness of being freely, voluntarily united to Him and to each other in an ecstasy of love and delight compared with which the most rapturous love between a man and a woman on this earth is mere milk and water. And for that they've got to be free. Of course God knew what would happen if they used their freedom the wrong way: apparently, He thought it worth the risk. If God thinks this state of war in the universe a price worth paying for free will, that is, for making a real world in which creatures can do real good or harm and something of real importance can happen instead of a toy world which only moves when He pulls the strings, then we may take it as worth paying."

Love is only pure and true when it is practiced with free will and without coercion. Perhaps this is good strategy for those young (or young-at-heart) people who are trying to woo someone into loving them.

While meditating about chapter three in Genesis, the Lord seems to speak to me concerning a perspective we often overlook; that is Adam remaining by her side. He did not forsake Eve during her lapse of judgement. To clarify this further, Adam loved Eve so much that he remained by her side even as God is chastising the both of them. This is commendable because it shows how much love Adam had for Eve.

However, there is more to this chapter than simply the two jilted lovers clinging together and getting kicked out of the Garden of Eden. This chapter, though it is simple and profound, is the most important chapter in the entire Bible. The message of this chapter is simple: if you disobey God's commandment, you have committed the act of sin.

We are told in Genesis chapter three that a certain cunning serpent entered the garden to tempt Eve to eat from the tree of the knowledge of good and evil. Although God had given both of them the liberty of eating food from every other tree in the garden, He commanded Adam and Eve not to eat from the tree of the knowledge of good and evil. With the words, "Has God indeed said you should not eat of every tree in the garden?" and later "you will not surely die", the serpent managed to convince Eve to break God's command. God's word, which is how everything is created and came to existence and is therefore powerful, was challenged by the serpent.

Genesis 3:1. Now the serpent was more cunning than any beast of the field which the Lord God had made. And he said to the woman, "Has God indeed said, 'You shall not eat of every tree of the garden'?"

Genesis 3:4. Then the serpent said to the woman, "You will not surely die.

Just to be emphatically clear, the serpent is usurping the authority of God's Word. Eve believed the serpent, ate the fruit, and then gave to Adam, who also ate of the fruit. This event was of grave consequence; it is known as the fall of mankind. It is understood by most Bible scholars that this event occurred after the heavenly event of Isaiah 14:12-21 and Ezekiel 28:11-15.

Isaiah 14:12. How you are fallen from heaven, O Lucifer, son of the morning! How you are cut down to the ground, You who weakened the nations!

13. For you have said in your heart: "I will ascend into heaven, I will exalt my throne above the stars of God; I will also sit on the mount of the congregation On the farthest sides of the north;

14. I will ascend above the heights of the clouds, I will be like the Most High."

15. Yet you shall be brought down to Sheol, To the lowest depths of the Pit.

16. Those who see you will gaze at you, And consider you, saying: "Is this the man who made the earth tremble, Who shook kingdoms,

17. Who made the world as a wilderness And destroyed its cities, Who did not open the house of his prisoners?"

18. All the kings of the nations, All of them, sleep in glory, Everyone in his own house;

19. But you are cast out of your grave Like an abominable branch, Like the garment of those who are slain, Thrust through with a sword, Who go down to the stones of the pit, Like a corpse trodden underfoot.

20. You will not be joined with them in burial, Because you have destroyed your land And slain your people. The brood of evildoers shall never be named.

21. Prepare slaughter for his children Because of the iniquity of their fathers, Lest they rise up and possess the land, And fill the face of the world with cities.

Ezekiel 11:11. Moreover the word of the Lord came to me, saying,

12. "Son of man, take up a lamentation for the king of Tyre, and say to him, 'Thus says the Lord God: "You were the seal of perfection, Full of wisdom and perfect in beauty.

13. You were in Eden, the garden of God; Every precious stone was your covering: The sardius, topaz, and diamond, Beryl, onyx, and jasper, Sapphire, turquoise, and emerald with gold. The workmanship of your timbrels and pipes Was prepared for you on the day you were created.

14. You were the anointed cherub who covers; I established you; You were on the holy mountain of God; You walked back and forth in the midst of fiery stones.

15 You were perfect in your ways from the day you were created, Till iniquity was found in you."

This is known as the fall of Lucifer, which is Satan, the serpent in the garden. This is paradise lost, and human history changes course. Now the world as they know it has changed! God judged Adam and Eve for disobeying His command and began the process of death. Adam and Eve began dying, spiritually at first and later physically, because of the fall. Without this significant event, the Bible would not make sense.

Moreover, our life would not make sense. The fall didn't just affect them; it affected every person born after them, and all were plunged into the carnal sin. This includes you and every human being you know. It is because of Adam's sin that death came into the world.

Romans 5:12. Therefore, just as through one man sin entered the world, and death through sin, and thus death spread to all men, because all sinned.

This serves as a great explanation as to the origin of death, as many scientists today could not explain why our body deteriorates. Even the author of Ecclesiastes denotes that God made man upright.

Ecclesiastes 7:29. Truly, this only I have found: That God made man upright, But they have sought out many schemes.

The fact that man was made upright is a reference to God creating man without flaws or in this case any moral blemish. But when death enters through the disobedience of man which is called sin, man is no longer just or upright. It is after man's disobedience of God's command, that their eyes were opened (Genesis 3:7), indicating that they now knew that they are no longer perfect.

Genesis 3:7. Then the eyes of both of them were opened, and they knew that they were naked; and they sewed fig leaves together and made themselves coverings.

Adam and Eve understood the severity of their actions when the Bible mentioned that they were naked and ashamed. Both were ashamed and tried to resolve their problem by covering themselves, which indicates evidence of a change in their condition. They were also ashamed, which is a condition caused by sinful nature.

Many theologians have focused on the manipulation and scheming of the serpent and credited his cunning method for deceiving Eve into disputing God's word. One can concede that Satan's deception focused on persuading Adam and his wife Eve to question God's promises and commands, as so many of us often get tempted to do the same on a daily basis. This idea is carried out in the New Testament.

1 John 2:16. For all that is in the world—the lust of the flesh, the lust of the eyes, and the pride of life—is not of the Father but is of the world.

However, we must also acknowledge that we have a greater power within us to resist the devil, and he has to flee.

The parallel to our lives when we disobey God is uncanny. It seems that at first, we experienced something similar in that we become anxious and concerned about whether or not God is looking out for our best interest. We encounter the readiness for us to believe a lie; this comes in a form of looking for circumstances to justify our disobedience.

Next, here comes the monster of lust, which is the craving to have and enjoy something we are not supposed to have, which is validated often by the needs of our flesh. Then comes rebellion; the outward expression of our inner desire. Often, we justify it by looking around for validation from others.

Third is the illusion of freedom, which is the mistaken notion that through sin we can experience the pleasure of life, a justification for our wrongdoing.

Then comes pride; pride in our new lifestyle and an arrogant disdain for those who try to do good and refuse to go along with us. Then there is anxiety; annoying fear that things aren't right, and underneath it all our lives are really on the brink of disaster. With anxiety, we feel the weight of sin burdening our shoulders, causing spiritual separation and even physical torment.

Upon closer scrutiny of the stages of disobedience, we see an obvious pattern. It can be broken down into various stages. The four stages shown will help us to understand what happened to Adam and Eve. It can happen and often does happen in our everyday struggles.

Let's take a closer look at the four stages of disobedience mentioned here. First we see in these verses that they were alienated from God. Adam and Eve disobeyed God and tried to hide from Him, and then when God questioned them about what they had done, they came up with excuses instead of confessing their sin and asking forgiveness of their sin, which separates from God.

Second, we see that Adam and Eve became alienated from one another. Their intense feeling of anxiety and guilt made them suspicious of each other. Love was replaced by desire, and physical desires are always a poor substitute for love. The word "desire" used here apparently refers to sexual desire. The relationship between a man and a woman would be clouded with uncertainty; it would lead either to fulfillment together or to failure together.

Third, there was also alienation between humans and animals, as symbolized by God's curse that the human race and the serpent would be enemies of each other. This curse will become the battle between God and Satan from this moment on.

As God and Adam with Eve began to play hide and seek, we encounter the chain of blame. When Adam blamed Eve, and Eve the serpent, we see the same pattern of justification that is practiced within the human race. Taking responsibility for your action is God's trait, not human; only the Holy Spirit can teach and do that for us.

Adam and Eve never showed self-awareness until this moment. However, sin opened their negative eyes and destroyed their innocence. Although Adam wasn't deceived and Eve was, they knew that they had both fallen into transgression.

1 Timothy 2:14. And Adam was not deceived, but the woman being deceived, fell into transgression.

Adam was blamed by Paul and others because he was the head of the household. Adam disobeyed God. He was responsible over the action of Eve; he should have resisted the temptation and deception of Satan by standing firm on the word of God. Adam caused the fall of the human race and placed us in need of redemption.

1 Corinthians 15:22. For as in Adam all die, even so in Christ all shall be made alive. 23. But each one in his own order: Christ the first fruits, afterward those who are Christ's at His coming.

In Genesis 3:14, God began to deal with the end of the blame chain, which is the serpent.

Genesis 3:14. So the Lord God said to the serpent: "Because you have done this, You are cursed more than all cattle, And more than every beast of the field; On your belly you shall go, And you shall eat dust All the days of your life.

He cursed it with the belly-rubbing, ground-crawling, humiliating existence that eventually will be crushed by the woman when her seed will bruise its head. **Now this is The First Good News!**

Genesis 3:15. And I will put enmity

Between you and the woman,

And between your seed and her Seed;

He shall bruise your head,

And you shall bruise His heel."

What is the first food news? Greek scholars coined the term as Protoevangelium. So, what is Protoevangelium? This compound word simply means the first gospel. *Protos* means "first" and *evangelion* means "good news" or gospel. The first gospel—the initial good news from God—can first be found within Genesis 3:15 according to Bible scholars.

This is the first messianic prophecy. The scripture tells us two concepts that are essential to the Christian worldview. First is that Satan (represented by the snake) and Christ (the seed of the woman) will be hostile to one another, which is enmity. Secondly, although Satan will bruise Christ's heel, Jesus will defeat Satan by bruising his head.

Adam's disobedience resulted in the curse of mankind. This resulted in sin in the world and thus in God's redemptive plan of salvation to restore mankind's ability to fellowship with Him. God did this by sending a messiah for the propitiation of our sins. The central theme of this book is to show that from the beginning of creation, God's plan is for us to have fellowship with Him and one another.

Genesis 3:21. Also for Adam and his wife the Lord God made tunics of skin, and clothed them.

Going along with this scripture, God will use His son, Jesus Christ, to redeem us from all of our sins. Christ will be the seed from the woman that will crush the head of Satan, the serpent. The power of Christ will destroy Satan and all of his principalities and power.

Jesus would die on the cross, crushing the devil's head forever, for the redemption of our sins. God always had a salvation redemption plan from the beginning, even as sin was introduced in the world.

Ephesians 6:12. For we do not wrestle against flesh and blood, but against principalities, against powers, against the rulers of the darkness of this age, against spiritual hosts of wickedness in the heavenly places.

God's redemption plan was revealed through the death and resurrection of His son, Jesus Christ. He is the sacrificial lamb depicted at the entrance of the garden also for the propitiation of our sins today.

1 John 3:8. He who sins is of the devil, for the devil has sinned from the beginning. For this purpose the Son of God was manifested, that He might destroy the works of the devil.

In summary, there will be a Savior, which is the seed of the woman, who will be the One that will conquer Satan and therefore conquer sin. Even though He, in the conquering, will be bruised, He will crush the deadly enemy. We will be victorious through Jesus Christ, our Lord and Savior.

God judged the devil by putting him on notice, and He warned him that his time was limited. In Genesis 3:15, we know that the woman represents God's chosen people, and her offspring the Seed is the Messiah. Although Satan, the serpent, will bruise the Messiah initially, the offspring will crush and defeat the Serpent once and for all.

Again for emphasis, this is Protoevangelium, which means the first good news or the first Gospel. The coming of Christ was first announced here, and redemption begins here. The Seed of the woman will become the eventual Redeemer, starting here in the Garden of Eden and ending with the pleading of the cup of suffering in the Garden of Gethsemane.

The Bible also speaks of the time when the animal world and human beings will eventually be reconciled to each other, and their relationship will be restored in paradise.

Romans 8:21. Because the creation itself also will be delivered from the bondage of corruption into the glorious liberty of the children of God.

Isaiah 11:6. The wolf also shall dwell with the lamb, The leopard shall lie down with the young goat, The calf and the young lion and the fatling together; And a little child shall lead them. 7. The cow and the bear shall graze; Their young ones shall lie down together; And the lion shall eat straw like the ox. 8. The nursing child shall play by the cobra's hole, And the weaned child shall put his hand in the viper's den. 9. They shall not hurt nor destroy in all My holy mountain, For the earth shall be full of the knowledge of the Lord As the waters cover the sea.

The fourth curse helps explain the nature of our world. God said to the woman, "I will greatly multiply your sorrow in your conception; in pain you shall bring forth children, your desires shall be for your husband, and he shall rule over you."

Then there was alienation between human beings and the soil that gave them food. Adam's disobedience caused the earth to be cursed in Genesis 3:17.

Genesis 3:17. Then to Adam He said, "Because you have heeded the voice of your wife, and have eaten from the tree of which I commanded you, saying, 'You shall not eat of it': Cursed is the ground for your sake; In toil you shall eat of it all the days of your life."

Cultivating the soil would no longer be a labor of love but a labor of sorrow and hard work. The soil would produce thorns and thistles as people struggled to make food. And lastly, our bodies would be reclaimed by the earth.

Genesis 3:18. "Both thorns and thistles it shall bring forth for you, And you shall eat the herb of the field. 19. In the sweat of your face you shall eat bread Till you return to the ground, For out of it you were taken; For dust you are, And to dust you shall return."

We are now living in a cursed world as a result of Adam's sin, and the curses affect all areas of our lives. The sufferings and pains are felt by the whole creation as described in Romans 8:18 and 23.

Romans 8:18. For I consider that the sufferings of this present time are not worthy to be compared with the glory which shall be revealed in us.

Romans 8:23. Not only that, but we also who have the first fruits of the Spirit, even we ourselves groan within ourselves, eagerly waiting for the adoption, the redemption of our body.

The Scriptures remind us that we need our Savior, who alone can fix our world by changing our hearts. Although death and sufferings are the enemy, our Lord Jesus came to heal the sick and raise the dead before he endured the cross and defeated death himself. He is our eternal hope of salvation. Jesus is called the "last Adam" in 1 Corinthians 15:45.

1 Corinthians 15:45. And so it is written, "The first man Adam became a living being." The last Adam became a life-giving spirit.

When Adam—God's appointment to the human race—sinned, he corrupted the human race, but Jesus will undo the corruption.

Romans 5:18. Therefore, as through one man's offense judgment came to all men, resulting in condemnation, even so through one Man's righteous act the free gift came to all men, resulting in justification of life.

It is within verse 16 that God begins to deal with the woman.

Genesis 3:16. To the woman He said: "I will greatly multiply your sorrow and your conception; In pain you shall bring forth children; Your desire shall be for your husband, And he shall rule over you."

God informed Eve of the coming struggle, the tugging of desire to be ruled by her man. As the serpent successfully deceived Eve, she did the same to Adam, thus usurping power from him. It is from this moment on that husband and wife would struggle to attain control over the relationship. Moreover, the happiest moment of a woman's life would be scarred by excruciating pain, which is child-birth. One can say that both feminism and chauvinism were rooted within this event.

Now that we know the bad news, we can begin working towards the healing process in order to possibly to have some good news.

Genesis 3:17. Then to Adam He said, "Because you have heeded the voice of your wife, and have eaten from the tree of which I commanded you, saying, 'You shall not eat of it': "Cursed is the ground for your sake; In toil you shall eat of it."

Now, God deals with the man, Adam. Noticed, starting with verse 17, God began to curse all the things that Adam used to enjoy doing. God cursed the ground, making it difficult for him to produce food. He didn't stop there; God also placed thorns and thistles to make it even more painstakingly frustrating to work the fields.

Believe me when I say, thorns and thistles are the worst to get rid of in the garden. Was that all? No, God even cursed Adam with death! So, from this moment on Adam will start experiencing the product or wage for his sin, which is spiritual and physical death. The consequences of the fall have seriously affected Adam and the rest of mankind. Death is inescapable by all men, and we will all be judged for our sin.

Hebrews 9:27. And as it is appointed for men to die once, but after this the judgment...

It is interesting to note that despite anger over what the pair of humans had done, God showed His mercy and grace. In verse 21, God probably killed a lamb, using a tunic of skin to clothe Adam and his wife, Eve, mother of all living.

Genesis 3:21. Also for Adam and his wife the Lord God made tunics of skin, and clothed them.

This explains why we wear clothes. This was also prophetic, as we see in Hebrews 9:22.

Hebrews 9:22. And according to the law almost all things are purified with blood, and without shedding of blood there is no remission.

John 1:29. The next day John saw Jesus coming toward him, and said, "Behold! The Lamb of God who takes away the sin of the world!"

Isaiah 53:1. Who has believed our report? And to whom has the arm of the Lord been revealed? 2. For He shall grow up before Him as a tender plant, And as a root out of dry ground. He has no form or comeliness; And when we see Him, There is no beauty that we should desire Him. 3. He is despised and rejected by men, A

Man of sorrows and acquainted with grief. And we hid, as it were, our faces from Him; He was despised, and we did not esteem Him. 4. Surely He has borne our griefs And carried our sorrows; Yet we esteemed Him stricken, Smitten by God, and afflicted. 5. But He was wounded for our transgressions, He was bruised for our iniquities; The chastisement for our peace was upon Him, And by His stripes we are healed.

About 2000 years ago, the first part of God's great rescue occurred. The true Lamb, which He promised through the Old Testament prophet Isaiah, was Jesus Christ. He died for the propitiation of our sin to make a way for us to be able to fellowship and be with God forever. All we have to do is repent and trust Him completely.

Then we are told of the banishment from the Garden of Eden. One can surely see the intent behind this occurrence, that God is protecting the human race in their depraved state of sinfulness. God did not allow them to stay in the Garden at the risk of them eating of the tree of life causing them to live forever in their imperfect state of being. His mercy was shown when the couple was driven out of the garden, but His salvation plan was already implemented. While Adam was to blame for his iniquity, God's redemption plan through the Seed He promised was in motion. When Jesus died on the cross, He declared it: *Tetelestai*, "It is finished."

John 19:30. So when Jesus had received the sour wine, He said, "It is finished!" And bowing His head, He gave up His spirit.

We only insult God when we try to add to His plan of salvation by our works or anything else.

Through Adam sin enters the world, but Jesus Christ offers us life eternal.

Our Father in heaven, we thank you for this plan of salvation for our lives. We are confident that from the beginning you have devised a plan of salvation to restore mankind to be able to have fellowship with you. Your plan of salvation by sending your only begotten Son, Jesus Christ, into this world is perfect and complete. We praise you and give you the glory and honor forever, Amen.

CHAPTER 4
THE BEGINNING OF THE EFFECTS OF SIN

Good News: Your biggest critic just left your church, pastor.

Bad News: He has been appointed the Head Bishop of your denomination.

Chapter three was significant because it describes for us the root of sin, but in chapter four we will see the outcome of the fruit of sinfulness. Although the book of Genesis spans 2500 years of history, this chapter and the next covers approximately 1500 years of it. After Adam and Eve were cast out of the garden, no one was able to return to this paradise until God's appointed time.

Again, chapter three is the root of sin, but chapter four is the fruit of sin. In chapter four, we begin with the miracle of a birth story. It seems that Adam "knew" his wife Eve and she conceived two sons name Cain and Abel. The Hebrew word for "knew" here means to know intimately. Adam and Eve enjoyed physical intimacy within the boundaries of marriage, just as God intended. Consequently, any act of physical intimacy that is not within the confines of man and woman in a marriage is just plain sexual immorality.

Imagine the amazement when they both experienced the miracle of birth. They bore Cain; the reference word here is "acquired". Eve named the child. This, she thought, was the seed that is referenced within Genesis 3:15. Eve bore another child named Abel. The couple put their hope into their children, but little did they know that one child would be a murderer. So it began: the downward spiraling of the fruit of sin.

Genesis 4:8. Now Cain talked with Abel his brother; and it came to pass, when they were in the field, that Cain rose up against Abel his brother and killed him.

The story of Cain and Abel leaves unanswered many of the questions that tantalize us, questions such as these: who taught Cain and Abel how to offer sacrifices? Why did God accept Abel's offering and reject Cain's? How did God show His approval of one offering and His disapproval of the other? What was the mark of Cain? Where was the land of Nod? Where did Cain get his wife? I am aware that as an apologist I am to offer you answers, not simply questions. Therefore, we will dig deep within the chapter and the rest of the scriptures to find the answers.

Although ancient cultures have alluded to the fact that most children are given a name by the man, in this case Eve gave Cain his name and said, "I have acquired a man from the Lord". Scholars have suspected that Eve thought that Cain was the Seed promised by God in 3:15 that would crush the head of the Serpent. In other words, Cain was going to be the "deliverer or anointed one" that would restore them back to paradise.

Eve's second child was named Abel, which means "breath" or "vapor". Maybe Eve hoped that Abel would be a wind beneath Cain's ascension into being the deliverer; a sort of support role for Cain. It is safe to presume that Eve could have favored Cain over Abel. Her notion was that Cain would be the great deliverer and Abel would become the spiritual support for his brother.

However, immediately, the Genesis writer has taken us on a roller coaster ride, it seems. The sibling rivalry has taken a grave turn. Cain and Abel were probably taught by their parents to worship God by giving Him homage of the fruits of their labor. Cain was a farmer and Abel was a shepherd; they gave according to what they had. Abel offered God "the first born of his flock and their fat", while Cain "the fruit of the ground".

The Lord "respected" Abel and his offering but rejected Cain's. It is noteworthy to point out that the difference in the mannerism of the offering between the best and the rest is what made God accept and reject the offerings. Able gave his best to God without regard to his own need, where Cain simply gave what he had left over. God always looks at the heart of the worshiper.

Hebrews 11:4. By faith Abel offered unto God a more excellent sacrifice than Cain, by which he obtained witness that he was righteous, God testifying over his gift: and by it he being dead yet speaks.

It was Abel's faith and heart that made his offering pleasing to the Lord. It is our duty to make sure that our actions are right and our hearts are in the right place. With God, it is important that we are humble in giving of the first fruits of our labor with a cheerful heart, understanding that such works themselves do not save us, and gladly accepting instructions, corrections, and even review from the hand of the Almighty.

Cain harbored anger and bitterness with his offering. He was a murderer in his heart way before he committed the act itself. We mirror this act as we see it in 1 John 3:12. Cain's works were evil and Abel was righteous.

1 John 3:12. ...not as Cain who was of the wicked one and murdered his brother. And why did he murder him? Because his works were evil and his brother's righteous.

Then in verse 8 it happened: the first sin outside the Garden of Eden.

Genesis 4:8. Now Cain talked with Abel his brother; and it came to pass, when they were in the field, that Cain rose up against Abel his brother and killed him.

He then arrogantly lied to God trying to deny his dirty deed. God still gave Cain a chance to confess his sin, but Cain continued to rebel. This shows the haughtiness of a murderer's mindset. God still showed mercy and gave Cain a chance to come clean. But when Cain said, "I do not know, am I my brother's keeper?" God confirmed that Cain had a hardened heart.

God's implied answer to the question is, "Yes, you are your brother's keeper." Just as God had instructed Adam to cultivate, protect, and multiply by filling the earth, He means for all of us to take care of one another, not harm each other.

As Cain refused to repent, God reminded him how Abel's blood cried out for justice. God cursed the earth and Cain with it by causing him to live as a nomad. According to ancient history, the worst fate for any person to suffer within a tribe is banishment from the safety of his village; it is a death sentence. The phrase "let the punishment fit the crime" is never more true than this instance. God is essentially pointing out, "Because you refused to become your brother's keeper, no one will be your keeper."

Then comes the pity plea of a desperate man. Cain complained to God that this punishment was too great for anyone to handle. He showed remorse but not repentance, in my opinion.

Genesis 4:13. And Cain said to the Lord, "My punishment is greater than I can bear!

This is similar to what some would term as "jailhouse repentance". We all have seen and heard those who get emotionally torn and regretfully teared only after they are caught.

2 Corinthians 7:10. For godly sorrow produces repentance leading to salvation, not to be regretted; but the sorrow of the world produces death.

Paul makes a clear distinction between true repentance and regretful remorse.

This brings us to the question of what "mark" God placed on Cain. Although the Bible doesn't clearly state, we can assume that God simply meant, "You are a marked man," and God continues to protect him undeservedly.

Genesis 4:15. And the Lord said to him, "Therefore, whoever kills Cain, vengeance shall be taken on him sevenfold." And the Lord set a mark on Cain, lest anyone finding him should kill him.

Cain skirted death and continue to grow his family. But how, you ask? Well, the Bible points out later in Genesis 5:4 that Adam had other children; it is logical to say that Cain came back and took his sister as a wife to grow his family. We will expound on this later in the book.

From a scientific point of view, the genetics of the very early humans were pure and perfect. It is sound science to believe that there was no anomaly that would cause this marriage to have any abnormality in reproduction.

When God had shown grace to Cain, Cain left and began to dwell in the land of Nod, which is east of Eden. The meaning of Nod was "a place of wandering" or "a place away from God". It is important to note that Cain married and had a son and built this city.

In Cain's family line, sin continues to grow. Even as God had spoken of a man leaving his family and joining himself to one wife (Genesis 2:24), Cain's family line took two wives. Although this practice soon became an accepted norm, it was never God's intention, and it became the root cause of troubled home life (Deuteronomy 21:15-17). This was clearly shown in the life of Lamech, who took two wives and bragged about his killing prowess. He was the first bigamist. He continued the trend of violence by taking revenge "seventy sevenfold" more than Cain's. This trend perhaps is what led to depravity of humanity that we see within Genesis 6:5-7.

Genesis 6:5. Then the Lord saw that the wickedness of man was great in the earth, and that every intent of the thoughts of his heart was only evil continually. 6. And the Lord was sorry that He had made man on the earth, and He was grieved in His heart. 7. So the Lord said, "I will destroy man whom I have created from the face of the earth, both man and beast, creeping thing and birds of the air, for I am sorry that I have made them."

Then we see hope emerge as we end the chapter. Adam knew his wife, Eve, again, and she bore a son called Seth. This third son would become the Godly line of succession, which explains why the Bible switched to Seth's line of succession. Through the line of Seth, God would send the promised Messiah.

Genesis 4:25. And Adam knew his wife again, and she bore a son and named him Seth, "For God has appointed another seed for me instead of Abel, whom Cain killed."

Adam and Eve obeyed God by continuing to populate the earth. They never lost the hope that their seed will produce the redeemer or messiah.

Genesis 4:26. And as for Seth, to him also a son was born; and he named him Enosh. Then men began to call on the name of the Lord.

Consequently, this generation of godly men is where we later find Noah's ancestors. Some translations suggest that men began to use the divine name Yahweh as they worshiped God. God's perfect redemption plan is beginning to become perfectly executed as we end the tragic chapter on a hope of the coming of the Messiah through the genealogy of Seth.

Heavenly Father, we give you the praise and honor to learn that your redemption hope continues with the line of Seth. We recognize that when sin knocks on our door, we should not answer it. We let the power of the Holy Spirit guide us to resist sin. We thank you for the power through your Son and our Savior Jesus. In His name we pray, amen.

CHAPTER 5
THE BEGINNING OF THE AGE OF MAN

Gallery Owner: I have some good news and some bad news.

Picasso: What's the good news?

Gallery Owner: The good news is that a man came in here today asking if the price of your paintings would go up after you die. When I told him they would he bought every one of your paintings.

Picasso: That's great! What's the bad news?

Gallery Owner: The bad news is that man was your doctor!

This chapter begins by giving us the genealogical list to Noah, who in essence stood in the tenth generation from Adam. The Bible's accurate historical method of using the genealogy list tells us that God has interest in timeline and accuracy. Perhaps God knows that the future depends upon the accuracy that he enables, to give us a good historical account of the age of the earth, which in turn gives us the age of the universe. Here the genealogy of Cain has been dropped and Seth's line of succession listed. The genealogy testifies to the blessings pronounced upon human beings in Genesis 1:28 being fulfilled.

Genesis 1:28. Then God blessed them, and God said to them, "Be fruitful and multiply; fill the earth and subdue it; have dominion over the fish of the sea, over the birds of the air, and over every living thing that moves on the earth."

The human family was multiplying and filling up the earth even as God instructed. God's plan all along is that we would fill the earth, and God the Creator loves all people in all times and is eager for everyone to receive the richness of life in Him that He freely offers.

The genealogy shows direct descendants from father to son; unlike the New Testament, it does not skip generations.

Genesis 5:5. So all the days that Adam lived were nine hundred and thirty years; and he died.

This is the fruit of sin. Noticeable facts here are the variety of names given to the firstborn sons and the very length of their lives. The genealogy focuses primarily on God's redemptive people.

Malachi 3:16. Then those who feared the Lord spoke to one another, and the Lord listened and heard them; so a book of remembrance was written before Him. For those who fear the Lord And who meditate on His name.

This leads us to a conversation about age and dating systems. What about the theory of ageism? If you look closely when Adam was created on day 6, he was one day old. In other words, he was a fully formed man; so was the universe. God created everything completely developed without the age factor. God created everything in its advanced form regardless of any chronological age dating method; they didn't look minutes old but months or years old.

This explains the planets also. It puts into perspective how planets that are light-years away are seen by humans on earth; God placed it there and it appeared. In addition, God began establishing the life cycle of every living thing; He caused it to reproduce, grow, and die. Even after a substantial number of years of living because of their near-perfect genetics, people died. Except for the rare occasion (Enoch walked with God and he was not…), death cast its shadow upon all men.

Genesis 5:24. And Enoch walked with God; and he was not, for God took him.

Enoch's famed experience echoed throughout the New Testament. Several passages refer to him, and in Hebrews 11 he is noted as one of the great men of faith.

Hebrews 11:5. By faith Enoch was taken away so that he did not see death, "and was not found, because God had taken him"; for before he was taken he had this testimony, that he pleased God. 6. But without faith it is impossible to please Him, for he who comes to God must believe that He is, and that He is a rewarder of those who diligently seek Him.

The Bible says that the church will experience a similar event in the future (1 Thessalonians 4:16-17).

1 Thessalonians 4:16. For the Lord Himself will descend from heaven with a shout, with the voice of an archangel, and with the trumpet of God. And the dead in Christ will rise first. 17. Then we who are alive and remain shall be caught up together with them in the clouds to meet the Lord in the air. And thus we shall always be with the Lord.

When Jesus descends to the atmosphere to gather His believers together with Him, every Christian alive on the earth at that time is taken to heaven. Perhaps Enoch's experience is a preview of what would be foretold later. According to the book of Jude, Enoch prophesied about the coming judgement upon his generation, to happen after Methuselah was born.

Jude 14. Now Enoch, the seventh from Adam, prophesied about these men also, saying, "Behold, the Lord comes with ten thousands of His saints, 15. to execute judgment on all, to convict all who are ungodly among them of all their ungodly deeds which they have committed in an ungodly way, and of all the harsh things which ungodly sinners have spoken against Him."

It's interesting to note that the Hebrew root word *muth* means "death" and *shellac* means "to bring" or "send". Methuselah means "his death shall bring," and we can see in the Bible that it was after his death that the flood happened. It was known that God's judgement upon the world was predicted, without surprise, four generations before it happened. God, through Enoch, gave a prophetic message through his son, Methuselah, about the impending doom. The year that Methuselah died is when the flood came.

This is precisely why the Bible states that Enoch began to walk closer to the Lord; Enoch knew of God's redemptive plan, given that his son's name reflected this divine judgement. Enoch knew of the impending doom of humankind, which caused him to walk closer to God, having a meaningful relationship with Him.

Moreover, Methuselah's longevity on earth was part of God's mercy and grace. God's redemptive plan was executed with patience and longsuffering, giving every opportunity for everyone to hear and listen to His warnings and repent from their wicked ways. This is the true *agape* love of our Creator. God's mercy endures forever.

Meanwhile, from Lamech, Methuselah's son, we know a man named Noah. From every blow of the hammer and every grind of his saw, we learn how God's redemptive plan was to unfold. The ark was a symbol of the promise of God's redemptive plan. God patiently brought the physical symbol to life for the world around Noah's generation to see, in hopes that they would repent and turn from their evil ways. God's judgement upon the world was coming, but His mercy and grace was shown through the physical manifestation of Noah's Ark.

The ages of death range from 365 years old for Enoch (Genesis 5:23) to 969 for Methuselah (Genesis 5:27). The average lifespan during this period was 857 years.

Genesis 5:23. So all the days of Enoch were three hundred and sixty-five years.

Genesis 5:27. So all the days of Methuselah were nine hundred and sixty-nine years; and he died.

The length of life described here isn't because times in those days were calculated differently. Instead, the length of their lives gives us a clue of what was possible for people before sin had penetrated so deeply into human experience. Consequently, science today supports the notion that our bodies were meant to live longer than we are living now. The current study of the human genome proves this is a possibility.

I would like to point out something else about Enoch, the one of whom the Genesis writer says "he was not; for God took him."

Genesis 5:24. And Enoch walked with God; and he was not, for God took him.

(This seems to suggest that Enoch was simply taken away without experiencing conventional death.) Again, it is worthy of explanation that Jude 14 later mentioned that Enoch was the seventh from Adam. This suggests that the genealogy was historically accurate without any gaps.

It's interesting to point out that there are more words about Enoch in the New Testament than in the Old Testament. Until the Flood, living to about 900 years old was considered as average. In addition, people like Enoch (or Elijah later on) were translated without dying.

This chapter goes in-depth about where we came from and who our ancestors were, and it could never be overlooked. If we realized what our heritage means and how important our ancient patriarchs are, we would learn to appreciate and have a better understanding of who we are and where we are going.

At the end of the chapter, we were given a glimpse of perhaps the most important historical figure in these early chapters, a man named Noah, who had three sons: Shem, Ham, and Japheth. The writer of Genesis is beginning to set the stage of the most important account about mankind's beginning in the concluding words of this chapter.

It is clear that Noah's story could only be understood in the light of the brief rehearsal of how sin had almost entirely taken control of the attitudes and actions of the people. The world continued to worsen because of sin. But this we will discuss in the next chapter.

Heavenly Father, we thank you for revealing your plan even from the beginning of time. You have shown us how Enoch knew of your redemptive plan to wipe away sins by naming his son Methuselah. We give you the glory and honor for giving us the insight into your scripture. We know that only the Holy Spirit can give us the full knowledge of what we read within the Bible. We pray that it changes our hearts to walk closer to you and help build your kingdom on earth as it is in heaven. We ask all this in Jesus' name, amen.

CHAPTER 6
THE BEGINNING OF JUDGEMENT

This is the story of a pastor who got up one Sunday and made an announcement to his congregation.

Pastor Jon Wixtrom: I have good news and bad news.

Congregation: Tell us the good news first, pastor.

Pastor Jon Wixtrom: The good news is we have enough money to pay for our new building program.

Congregation: Then what is the bad news?

Pastor Jon Wixtrom: The bad news is it's still in your pockets.

The two most awesome cataclysmic events in the Bible that would be the center of controversy among secular and Christian scholars alike are the creation of the universe and everything in it and the Great Flood. We have stated that the creation of the world and everything in it happened within six 24-hour days, but the flood lasted about 371 days. The creation process is fully matured. The Flood happened globally.

We will explore the chapter by answering some basic questions from a ten-year-old girl. What can we say about the sons of God and their relationship with the daughters of men? Why did God choose to wipe out humankind? Could there really be a global flood?

The chapter opens up with scriptures that have many Bible scholars arguing the meaning behind "sons of God" and "daughters of men". If you wish to seek further guidance, there is a great article by Lee Anderson titled *Is the "Sons of God" Passage in Genesis 6 Adapted Pagan Mythology?* dated May 20, 2015.

Scholars suggest that there are three different interpretations to resolve the dilemma of the acts of "the sons of God with daughters of men". One is that the "sons of God" were fallen angelic beings that populated with human women and produced babies called *Nephilim* in Hebrew, which means "fallen ones".

The second interpretation is that this simply refers to the line of Seth marrying the ungodly line of Cain. The "sons of God" are from Seth and "daughters of men" would be from Cain, making them Sethites mixing with Cainites.

The third is the view that depicts despotic rulers who married women, thus enlarging their harem. Although one can support each theory as an argument, I will offer biblical supporting evidence to prop up the first theory.

Jude 1:6. And the angels who did not keep their proper domain, but left their own abode, He has reserved in everlasting chains under darkness for the judgment of the great day.

The interpretation that the fallen angels of God were committing sexual immorality with the daughters of men is the oldest exegetical position.

1 Peter 3:18. For Christ also suffered once for sins, the just for the unjust, that He might bring us to God, being put to death in the flesh but made alive by the Spirit, 19. by whom also He went and preached to the spirits in prison, 20. who formerly were disobedient, when once the Divine longsuffering waited in the days of Noah, while the ark was being prepared, in which a few, that is, eight souls, were saved through water.

Peter seems to suggest that Christ went to preach to the disobedient, even during the construction of the Ark during Noah's days.

2 Peter 2:4. For if God did not spare the angels who sinned, but cast them down to hell and delivered them into chains of darkness, to be reserved for judgment 5. and did not spare the ancient world, but saved Noah, one of eight people, a preacher of righteousness, bringing in the flood on the world of the ungodly;

This is about the punishment to those angels who sinned and were later thrown into the pits of darkness.

Genesis 4:4. There were giants on the earth in those days, and also afterward, when the sons of God came in to the daughters of men and they bore children to them. Those were the mighty men who were of old, men of renown.

The freakish giants' presence roaming the earth as a result of the unholy union before the great flood leads to a problem mentioned in Numbers 13:33.

Numbers 13:33. There we saw the giants (the descendants of Anak came from the giants); and we were like grasshoppers in our own sight, and so we were in their sight.

From an apologetics viewpoint, it is important to note that the core of this chapter is the fact that men and women are displaying wickedness throughout the earth. It is assuring to know that "sons of God" (in Hebrew *bene Ha'Elohim*) usually exclusively refers to the fallen angels. The interpretation of them being angels is one better supported even within the scripture; as a biblical presupposition thinker, this writer would have to take a stand with that interpretation, which has generally been accepted by many Jewish scholars and conservative Bible scholars.

There is still the question as to why angels and human females would want to marry or conjugate with each other. These verses may give us some possible reasons. First, it was because the sons of God saw the daughters of men, that they were beautiful.

Genesis 6:2. that the sons of God saw the daughters of men, that they were beautiful; and they took wives for themselves of all whom they chose.

The implication here is that sons of God lusted after the daughters of men.

A second reason could be that humans wished to avoid the death penalty incurred by the Adam's sin curse. They wanted to live forever, and by creating a super race resulting from the intermarriage of angels and human beings, they might conceivably have thought they could accomplish this.

Nevertheless, whatever the reason, the attempt was to defy God and His Word. This obviously contributed to the great wickedness. Because of the supreme arrogance of God-created beings in striving to be like Him, wickedness and evil was no longer confined to the earth itself but was now prevalent throughout heaven and earth. Perhaps this could explain why God was sorry that He had made them.

Then God showed His redemption plan in 6:8, stating that He had found someone to shed his grace upon. So now, looking back into the midst of this repulsive wickedness, we meet a righteous man who seems to stand out in bold relief in Genesis 6:8-10.

Genesis 6:8. But Noah found grace in the eyes of the Lord. 9. This is the genealogy of Noah. Noah was a just man, perfect in his generations. Noah walked with God. 10. And Noah begot three sons: Shem, Ham, and Japheth.

He was a just man, in Hebrew *tamim* (which means filled with moral integrity) and even perfect in his generation, having a characteristic of walking with God. God saw the righteousness in this man named Noah; he found grace in the eyes of the Lord. Then we begin witnessing God's horrifying response to mankind's wickedness.

Genesis 6:13. And God said to Noah, "The end of all flesh has come before Me, for the earth is filled with violence through them; and behold, I will destroy them with the earth.

With a sense of urgency, God continues to devise a plan. This plan includes rescuing and rebuilding the world through Noah and his family.

Matthew 24:37. But as the days of Noah were, so also will the coming of the Son of Man be.

Within Romans, we can get a sense of what the world would have been like in the days of Noah. The pre-flood days were filled with all things wicked in the eyes of God. There were, according to Noah, no seekers of God detected in the pre-flood world.

Romans 1:20. For since the creation of the world His invisible attributes are clearly seen, being understood by the things that are made, even His eternal power and Godhead, so that they are without excuse, 21. because, although they knew God, they did not glorify Him as God, nor were thankful, but became futile in their thoughts, and their foolish hearts were darkened. 22. Professing to be wise, they became fools, 23. and changed the glory of the incorruptible God into an image made like corruptible man—and birds and four-footed animals and creeping things. 24. Therefore God also gave them up to uncleanness, in the lusts of their hearts, to dishonor their bodies among themselves, 25. who exchanged the truth of God for the lie, and worshiped and served the creature rather than the Creator, who is blessed forever. Amen. 26. For this reason God gave them up to vile passions. For even their women exchanged the natural use for what is against nature. 27. Likewise also the men, leaving the natural use of the woman, burned in their lust for one another, men with men committing what is shameful, and receiving in themselves the penalty of their error which was due. 28. And even as they did not like to retain God in their knowledge, God gave them over to a debased mind, to do those things which are not fitting; 29. being filled with all unrighteousness, sexual immorality, wickedness, covetousness, maliciousness; full of envy, murder, strife, deceit, evil-mindedness; they are whisperers, 30. backbiters, haters of God, violent, proud, boasters, inventors of evil things, disobedient to parents, 31. undiscerning, untrustworthy, unloving, unforgiving, unmerciful; 32. who, knowing the righteous judgment of God, that those who practice such things are deserving of death, not only do the same but also approve of those who practice them.

Jesus compared His second coming to the great global flood of Noah. We are certain that this event will be catastrophic, not mere local disasters as some lack-luster teachers have proclaimed.

The Bible describes the antediluvian time as depraved. "Antediluvian" is a period before the flood, and the wickedness (in Hebrew *rah*) of man was very bad. God was grieved. This is an example of what may be called anthropopathy, the ascription of human passions or feelings to a being or beings not human, especially to a deity such as God.

We can see that our own worldwide conditions are a ripening indicator that the time of tribulation, which Jesus predicted, could be coming soon. While sexual immorality has been around for ages, it is more prevalent in our society and current generation. Sexual immorality is no longer practiced in secret or with some degree of shame; it is now being endorsed as mainstream. From bestiality to pedophilia, sexual immorality is taken to such an extreme that premarital sex has become an accepted norm among young people and even Christians. When I see programing within mainstream television and cable, I see an overwhelming majority of shows contain sexual depravity and immorality. Not to mention the lowering of standards, with sexual practice among young kids—as young as ten years old—in our society. Pornography, being a number-one problem among Christian and secular society alike, has become a billion-dollar industry.

Does this sound like the "as in the days of Noah" phrase? Wake up, Christians, and repent, so that the blood of Christ can cleanse you of all unrighteousness!

Noah found grace in the eyes of God. Noah was just, which is to mean he was filled with moral integrity. This man, Noah, walked with God. To this day, there are many cultures that speak of a morally upright man named Noah (or a variation of the name depending on culture or language origin).

Noah's righteousness was the reason his family was saved, including his three sons, Shem, Ham, and Japheth, along with their wives. We will discuss the fate of Noah's three sons in the latter chapter of this book. They became central in the building of the nations in the world. So, as God planned to destroy the earth, He began to make preparations to save Noah and his family.

God instructed Noah to build an ark made from gopher wood with the precise measurements to accommodate all that he was going to protect. God told him to make rooms in the ark and cover inside and outside with pitch, to resist water and seal it. The length of it was to be 300 cubits. The ark's width was fifty cubits and its height thirty cubits.

Noah needed to understand the displacement of solid objects. Displacement is the occupation by a submerged body or part of a body of a volume which would otherwise be occupied by a fluid. In other words, being able to take a solid object and its weight, and then dispersing it with the correct number of air-pockets in order to float on water or not have fluid occupy the air space. That is my basic level of explanation of the science of boat building.

According to our standard measurement today, this ship would be 450 feet long, that's one and a half football fields long. The width would be 75 feet wide, that's seven parking spaces, and it would be 45 feet tall, equal to four-story building. According to Bible experts, the space is calculated to be 100,000 square feet of deck space in the ark with three decks spaced fifteen feet apart. There would be 1.4 million cubic feet of storage space in that ship.

Why such detailed blueprints, you might ask? Could it be that Noah lacked the knowledge of boat building? Perhaps this was a huge project to undertake. Noah had never undertaken this monumental task before.

I have visited the Ark Encounter, a place where they have built a replica model of the original ark in Kentucky. It was mesmerizing to see the sheer magnitude of this massive boat.

Genesis 6:16. You shall make a window for the ark, and you shall finish it to a cubit from above; and set the door of the ark in its side. You shall make it with lower, second, and third decks.

This would serve as a way to collect rain water for survival, and even to get rid of the stale smell from inside the ark. God was bringing the floodwaters on the earth to destroy every living thing, "but He will spare you and your family" (speaking to Noah). "I will establish my covenant with you."

This worldwide flood—not just local—would consume the world and everything wicked. According to Whitcomb and Morris in their book *The Genesis Flood*, there could have been upward of 774 million to one billion people on the earth during this time. This was an enormous number of souls that could have been saved, yet only eight survived. Let us pause a moment and consider the gravity of this event.

Through Noah, God established a covenant. It is important to note that this is the first time God mentions the word "covenant".

Genesis 6:18. But I will establish My covenant with you; and you shall go into the ark—you, your sons, your wife, and your sons' wives with you.

The word covenant is an important concept throughout scripture. It comes from the Hebrew word *berit* which means an agreement. It is a binding agreement between God and humankind.

Today, there are many forms of agreement between parties involved; in fact, some are even made between objects and people. However, in the scriptures, there are only two types of covenants. The two types of covenants are called "parity" and "suzerainty". Parity simply means equal; a party of equals may want to agree. Suzerainty is an agreement between a superior over an inferior. For example, a king agreeing with a vassal state would be termed a suzerainty agreement.

The covenant that God made with Noah is this kind of covenant, and in this case it's not conditional. As we delve deep within the scriptures, we will see more of this type of covenant.

Genesis 6:19. And of every living thing of all flesh you shall bring two of every sort into the ark, to keep them alive with you; they shall be male and female. 20. Of the birds after their kind, of animals after their kind, and of every creeping thing of the earth after its kind, two of every kind will come to you to keep them alive. 21. And you shall take for yourself of all food that is eaten, and you shall gather it to yourself; and it shall be food for you and for them.

According to Whitcomb and Morris, during the antediluvian period there were about 17,600 species of land animals. This would include mammals, amphibians, and birds. Since the Bible mentions male and female, then we would have to double it to more than 35,000 spaces needed in the ark. If we add the clean animals needed for sacrifice, then it could be upward of 79,000. The ark could accommodate, according to Morris and Whitcomb, 125,000 sheep-size animals.

There was plenty of room in the ark for all the animals God wanted Noah to gather. However, that brings up another dilemma: how did Noah manage to round up all the animals into the ark? This is an easy answer: God called all the animals to come to Noah and they listened. Unlike humans, animals' free will depends upon their instinct, not spirit, as we discussed before. This speaks truth to me.

He would show mercy upon humankind in order that He could fulfill His salvation plan. It seems that this plan of wiping out humankind with rain and water from beneath the earth is laughable to most of the people in this generation, but Noah faithfully obeyed God.

Hebrews 11:7. By faith Noah, being warned of God of things not seen as yet, moved with fear, prepared an ark to the saving of his house; by the which he condemned the world, and we can share of the righteousness which is by faith.

In the history of humankind in over 217 nations or ethnic groups, you have flood stories. It's not just a biblical story. You have that record in almost every part of the world from South America to the different ethnic groups in Africa, even to the aborigines in Australia. The Hawaiian ancient story of Nuuh and his family can be traced back to Noah. There is also the Gilgamesh epic or the Babylonian flag, which is probably the most famous and closest to our biblical narrative; there are 270+ records of a worldwide flood that have existed through time.

In Noah's account of the global flood lies a great lesson learned as it relates to obeying God and God's faithfulness. Noah is obedient to follow the will of God. Here's a good example of a man who remains faithful and preaches the gospel of salvation from the flood for decades without wavering against the worst kinds of sins and evil that were practiced on earth. Noah stood unwavering despite the lack of support from even his closest relatives. He remained faithful to God's message of salvation by building the ark allowing even room for those who would change from their wicked ways and accept God's plan of salvation.

Noah witnessed to them and urged them to reject their evil ways and turn to God. This happened for almost 120 years, but the people rejected his message because they rejected God. However, Noah and his family were saved.

Noah would offer a sacrifice after he was rescued to give thanks to the Lord. God's plan had made provision for a sacrificial offering without endangering the food supply for Noah and his family. It is fitting that the chapter ends with

...thus Noah did; according to all that God commanded him, so he did. (Genesis 6:22)

Where are the "Noahs" of today, who would stand among the unbelieving world? Today's depraved world needs Noah's message of redemption and turning away from evil before all get drowned in their sin. Get on board from the only door to the ark, which is Jesus Christ our Lord.

John 10:9. I am the door. If anyone enters by Me, he will be saved, and will go in and out and find pasture.

Heavenly Father, I pray for the reader of this message to understand the depravity of human sins. Lord, your wish is not for anyone to perish but for everyone to accept your redemption message. The redemption message is this. God has sent his Son to die on the cross to repay the debt of sin; if we believe in Him, we will not perish but have everlasting life. I pray that everyone who reads this believe and repent. Thank you for your grace and mercy; I pray in Jesus name, amen.

CHAPTER 7
THE BEGINNING OF THE GLOBAL FLOOD

Dr. Kumlish Patell: I have some good news and some bad news.

Patient: Give me the bad news first, doc.

Doctor: So sorry to tell you, I'm afraid you have a genetic disease. Your DNA is backwards.

Patient: AND?

In chapter seven, we are faced with the ark completed and ready to be occupied. This is the first time you will find the word "come" appearing in the Bible; it's an invitation by God saying to come now.

Genesis 7:1. Then the Lord said to Noah, "Come into the ark, you and all your household, because I have seen that you are righteous before Me in this generation."

This isn't the only time; you will read several invitations that are like that throughout the scripture. One example is in Isaiah chapter one.

Isaiah 1:18. "Come now, and let us reason together," Says the Lord, "Though your sins are like scarlet, They shall be as white as snow; Though they are red like crimson, They shall be as wool."

This is all because Noah walked with God, just like Enoch did. He worked with God, and later in chapter eight, he gave an altar offering of worship to God. In a world of millions, even with the constant mocking from neighbors and friends, Noah stayed true to God's word. If you dare to defy the world and be a nonconformist, then be like Noah. After 120 years of mercy warning, God's judgement was upon humankind. In verse four, God warns Noah that he has seven days to load into the boat.

Genesis 7:4. For after seven more days I will cause it to rain on the earth forty days and forty nights, and I will destroy from the face of the earth all living things that I have made."

When the door of the ark made its last shutting sound with a thud, at the age of 600 Noah obeyed God in every aspect of His Word.

The validity of the science in this event may arise: could this be just a local flood? The answer again is no, because both the effort for the preservation of life and the subsiding of waters within 274 days could not account for it being just a local flood. Even if some insist that Noah was simply describing what he could see from his limited scope of view on the earth, a local flood doesn't destroy all people. The plain reading of the Bible is clear that God's judgement was global.

Keep in mind that people and continents hadn't shifted to where we find them today. The dispersion of populations would not happen until later within the

Bible. The populations of the earth were still confined within the central area of the earth.

Genesis 6:7. So the Lord said, "I will destroy man whom I have created from the face of the earth, both man and beast, creeping thing and birds of the air, for I am sorry that I have made them."

There is nothing within that scripture that suggests only a local flood. The extensive language written by God makes it clear that it was a global flood. Let's jump forward a little; we can see in the grammatical context that the writer emphasized the global nature of the flood.

Genesis 7:18. The waters prevailed and greatly increased on the earth, and the ark moved about on the surface of the waters.

It is important to note that in reading the Bible, you must approach it as literal, grammatical and historical.

We approach the Bible literally because it is straightforward with its plain, common language. We read it for what it says and what it is. It is taken literally unless otherwise demanded by a clear representation that is figurative language which would be easy to see as metaphor or simile.

We also understand it contextually according to the grammar functions in the sentence. We take into account the grammar of how the noun corresponds to the verb and subject to the object.

Furthermore, we take it historically; it is what it says it is. The structure of the book of Genesis suggests that it follows a chronological account of historical events, which would be the very definition of "history". This is the same pattern that we read and understand in other books of the Bible, such as Matthew, Acts, Romans, Isaiah, and Jeremiah, just to mention a few.

It is flabbergasting to find that when it comes to Genesis, scholars want to complicate the way we interpret. They want to reconcile it to man's theory or scientific discovery to confirm their own theories, whether it's a theory of billions of years, or local flood or the lack thereof. Genesis' chapters are straightforward, easy to read, and easy to understand. There was a big global flood, and that is how we read it.

Genesis 7:10. And it came to pass after seven days that the waters of the flood were on the earth. 11. In the six hundredth year of Noah's life, in the second month, the seventeenth day of the month, on that day all the fountains of the great deep were broken up, and the windows of heaven were opened.

With the impending flood that would last forty days and forty nights, Noah and his family had seven days to get everything loaded into the enormous ark. During the last week, Noah must have been in awe with trepidation of what was to come. However, there was still not a drop of rain. Noah, his wife, his three sons Shem, Ham, and Japhet along with their wives, and the specific animals were all secured in the in giant boat.

We have talked about how the animals were gathered into the ark; God simply called them. The Bible makes a specific reference as to how many animals and kinds.

Genesis 7:14. ...they and every beast after its kind, all cattle after their kind, every creeping thing that creeps on the earth after its kind, and every bird after its kind, every bird of every sort. 15. And they went into the ark to Noah, two by two, of all flesh in which is the breath of life. 16. So those that entered, male and female of all flesh, went in as God had commanded him; and the Lord shut him in.

The Bible does not specifically state how many kinds or what it means by "kinds"; therefore, some have tried inserting their interpretation of the scripture. Nevertheless, we can study the scripture and make educated guesses about what it really means based on biblical evidence. One will find what would agree with the science of biology and its basic principles. The Hebrew word used for kind is *min*, and we know that to create is *bara*. Therefore *baramin* is a creation term coined for "created kind".

The basic understanding of "created kinds" would be similar to "family" in the animal classification system. This is due to the functionality of reproductive nature. In case we have forgotten, the animal kingdom classifications or taxonomy are (1) Kingdom; (2) Phylum or Division; (3) Class; (4) Order; (5) Family; (6) Genus; (7) Species.

Although some experts conjecture "kind" to mean species and use it as an argument for the improbability of the event, this conjecture does not offer perspicuity of the scripture. The contextual meaning and idea of preserving the animals is for their reproductive process. It is not necessarily the same species. For example, crossing between dogs and wolves, wolves and coyotes, and coyotes and jackals goes to show that all these species of animals belong to a single family. The same created kind, in Hebrew *baramin*, can reproduce.

The reproduction process can be complex with sufficient barriers. We could make arguments regarding hybrids that would present valid scientific data and conclusions. However, this is not that moment. If you wish to dig deeper into hybrid reproduction, there are many scientific data that can prove its plausibility. "Answers in Genesis" offers many articles to support the biblical proof. One can agree that the straightforward meaning of this scripture is that God wanted to preserve the animal according to kinds, not species. It was for the sole purpose of repopulating the earth.

Suddenly the door began to close, allowing God's plan to unveil. As the waters began to pour from the heavens above and the earth below, the flood began to fill the earth. Again, Noah was 600 years old when the rain came.

Genesis 7:11. In the six hundredth year of Noah's life, in the second month, the seventeenth day of the month, on that day all the fountains of the great deep were broken up, and the windows of heaven were opened. 12. And the rain was on the earth forty days and forty nights.

Even as the great deep was spilling up from below, the windows of heaven opened, releasing torrents of rain. This great catastrophe scene must have been reminiscent of the state of chaos described in Genesis 1:2.

It is interesting to note that the Genesis writer took the time to give us Noah's age when they all entered the ark; this validates the book's historical account of this great catastrophic event. This historical account of the earth being torn apart and shaken like an ice blender can be confirmed today by seeing geologic findings and earth's divided continents. This is the greatest cataclysmic event that ever happened to earth since the creation. During any storm especially as devastating as this, I would rather be with God than anywhere else without God.

Upon reading, we learned that the water poured up out of the ground and the rain fell, causing the flood water to rise higher and higher.

Genesis 7:19. And the waters prevailed exceedingly on the earth, and all the high hills under the whole heaven were covered. 20. The waters prevailed fifteen cubits upward, and the mountains were covered.

Eventually, those floodwaters covered even the highest of mountains by a depth of roughly twenty-one and a half feet. The devastation was complete, as every living thing on the face of the earth died.

Being a surfer from the island of Hawaii, I know the devastating power of crashing water and waves; this is massive. Although God took the time to explain the geological devastation upon the earth, we must understand that the deep message of this catastrophic event is that every living thing was destroyed because God judged sin. This is perhaps why people have tried to diminish or at least lighten the message of the flood. Skeptics dismiss the seriousness of God's judgement upon humankind. They don't want to believe in a God that would ultimately judge the world for its sin by causing everyone on earth to die.

God is merciful and patient, but God's judgment was executed upon the world. God's initial warning 120 years before was met with blatant disregard; now the time had come for Him to judge man.

Genesis 7:21. And all flesh died that moved on the earth: birds and cattle and beasts and every creeping thing that creeps on the earth, and every man. 22. All in whose nostrils was the breath of the spirit of life, all that was on the dry land, died.

It is very clear that God's judgement was final because man's sin was severe.

We have other questions from skeptics about the animals and their accommodation within the ark. How did Noah fit all of those millions of species of animals into the ark? Did he have to feed them all?

We have dealt with the issue of kinds rather than species. Since this is the case, the different kinds (not species) that were loaded into the ark would be about 700. We need to understand that only land animals were needed for preservation within the ark, not sea creatures. The ark's measurements equate to 522 train box cars; studies show that 12 six-foot-long cows can fit into one 36-foot box car. Therefore, we can deduce there are plenty of rooms inside the ark for all the kinds of animals to fit.

My empirical experience of visiting the Ark Encounter, which is a life-size replica of the ark, confirms more than enough accommodation for Noah and his family members to live comfortably within the ark even with all 700 kinds of animals living inside. Indeed, this is a functioning, living zoo floating on water.

It also solidifies the notion that it can't be just a local flood, because a massive ship would not be necessary; they could have just moved when they heard the warning 120 years before. But in this boat, Noah and his family with all the animals were preserved. God is merciful.

The observable proofs of this event seen within the study of the science of geology. From geologic points of view, the global flood explains the natural existence of large inland seas in China, India, and the Great Basin in Nevada and Utah. It also explains the fossil records that show sea life that doesn't now exist anywhere near the places these fossils have been found. Fossilized fish, whales, and even sharks have been found in Wyoming, Michigan, and Ohio, which have elevations of around 7000 feet above sea level.

Massive forests were compressed by water pressure, as seen in the layers of water-laid deposits forming coal. Coal can be found near both North and South Poles. Geologists have found 9000 different animals buried by water and dirt in Agate Springs, Nebraska, encased in a great slab of sediments. This geologic anomaly can only be caused by a massive water event, which is the great global flood.

Then my 10-year-old asks the obvious question: Where did the waters come from?

Genesis 7:11. In the six hundredth year of Noah's life, in the second month, the seventeenth day of the month, on that day all the fountains of the great deep were broken up, and the windows of heaven were opened.

Literally speaking, it came from everywhere. The water came from the sky and from the ground. Scientists who hold the "Canopy Theory" have stated that the amount would be equal to 2.5 percent of the water that exist today. Let me expound a little on the Canopy Theory. It is based on interpretation of the "waters above" passage within Genesis 1:6-7.

Genesis 1:6. Then God said, "Let there be a firmament in the midst of the waters, and let it divide the waters from the waters." 7. Thus God made the firmament, and divided the waters which were under the firmament from the waters which were above the firmament; and it was so.

The model has attempted to explain where the water could have derived from, which is why there was a large amount causing the global flood. This theory seems to give a sound scientific explanation of the conditions of the earth's atmosphere, with a global covering shielding from the sun. Perhaps it would explain the long lifespan of man during the antediluvian period.

However, as researchers began to insert the data within a computer, it didn't work. The model proved that the latent heat of condensation would have boiled the atmosphere. In addition, it is not certain that there would have been enough water within the atmosphere to cause rain for forty days and forty nights. Moreover, the Bible seems to allude to the heavens still holding water.

Psalms 148:4. Praise Him, you heavens of heavens, And you waters above the heavens!

Therefore, many have abandoned this model. Further scientific study is needed to provide the best explanation for this event. For now, we will hold onto a basic understanding of the scripture to say that God caused the cataclysmic event supernaturally.

That is a massive amount of water. When God said, "all the fountains of the great deep were broken up," it explains the subterranean geological catastrophe that caused the tectonic rupture and shift. This geological event created separation on the earth, causing a divide within the earth's surface structure and thus creating what we know today as continents.

A quick Google search led me to a Creation.com article titled, "Analysis of Walt Brown Model" by Michael J. Ord. It offers an explanation of Dr. Brown's Hydro Plate Theory. He offers an explanation of the earth's cavernous structure that caused the water to come from the ground. In the antediluvian period, pressure built up in the subterranean chambers so that water burst forth at the beginning of the Flood. Brown theorized that this explains the eruption of the subterranean water, with the "fountains of the great deep" as the primary source of water for the global flood. Brown added that we can even date this event from the astronomical study of the universe.

It is noteworthy that Dr. Brown was an evolutionist until he began to study about the astronomical theory of the global flood; now he is a creationist. Since retiring from the military, Dr. Brown has been the Director of the Center for Scientific Creation and has worked full-time in research, writing, and teaching on creation and the flood. He and many other creationist geologists suggest that there was water under the earth that God caused to erupt. This is the best explanation of where most of the water could have come from to cause the great worldwide flood. The validity of the historical account can be traced using Brown's Hydro Plate Model, tracing geological movements back to the days of Noah.

Even after the rain stopped, there was so much water that it lingered for many days.

Genesis 7:24. And the waters prevailed on the earth one hundred and fifty days.

Many scholars and scientists believe that the mountains were not as high as they are today, and the waters rose about twenty-two feet above them. They contend that the tectonic shift caused the mountains to rise higher.

However, the underlying message here is not geologic transformation, but rather God's judgement upon sin.

2 Peter 3:5. For this they willfully forget: that by the word of God the heavens were of old, and the earth standing out of water and in the water, 6. by which the world that then existed perished, being flooded with water. 7. But the heavens and the earth which are now preserved by the same word, are reserved for fire until the day of judgment and perdition of ungodly men.

Genesis 7:23. So He destroyed all living things which were on the face of the ground: both man and cattle, creeping thing and bird of the air. They were destroyed from the earth. Only Noah and those who were with him in the ark remained alive.

As much destruction as this chapter exudes, God shows mercy through preservation of His creation and His people. The geology is not as important as the theology of God's message. The message of this chapter is this. God saved Noah and his family, and His plan of salvation through them is still in the works. Within the ark lies the hope of the Messiah and God's fulfillment of His eternal restoration of the fellowship between Him and His people. To serve as a reminder of God's plan of salvation, we remember Genesis 3:15.

And I will put enmity

Between you and the woman,

And between your seed and her Seed;

He shall bruise your head,

And you shall bruise His heel.

In the next chapter we will see Gods redemptive plan carried out through Noah and his family. We will learn in chapter eight the meaning behind the words "God remembered Noah".

Dear heavenly Father, we know that you are the just God and your judgement is right and fair. We thank you that your mercy is everlasting and through your Son, Jesus, you have provided a way for us to reconcile our sin. You have provided a plan of redemption in order for us to return to fellowship with you through Christ. We thank you for that plan of redemption and we give you the glory and honor; we praise you for your eternal mercy, amen.

CHAPTER 8
THE BEGINNING OF A NEW WORLD

Long John Silver: I have bad news and good news.

Buccaneers: Bad news first, arrgh.

Long John Silver: My obese parrot died yesterday. However, there is some good news.

Buccaneers: What is the good news, arrgh?

Long John Silver: It's a lot of weight off my shoulders.

The chapter begins with Noah and those who were with him being sheltered from the storm in the ark. Then, the rain stopped.

The ark saved Noah and his family by staying afloat in the massive ocean of flood rain. Then God remembered Noah and everything that was inside the ark.

Genesis 8:1. Then God remembered Noah, and every living thing, and all the animals that were with him in the ark. And God made a wind to pass over the earth, and the waters subsided.

Bible scholars agree that this doesn't mean that God forgets things. That idea is simply ludicrous. Rather, now God began to focus on Noah. "Remembered" is just a way to describe in human terms the process of God's attention turning from the cataclysmic event of the flood to Noah's fate. The Hebrew verb used in this passage is *zakar* which means "to remember," and it is used 73 times in scriptures. It's a combination of memory with an action. God's focus is now turned to decreasing the water level and calming it in order for Noah to safely exit out of the ark.

Underneath the ark are millions of dead people and animals. What is now required is a massive decrease of water from the surface of the earth in order for the earth to be able to repopulate. Humans and animals have to be able to thrive in this new environment.

Genesis 8:2. The fountains of the deep and the windows of heaven were also stopped, and the rain from heaven was restrained. 3. And the waters receded continually from the earth. At the end of the hundred and fifty days the waters decreased.

Psalm 104:5. You who laid the foundations of the earth, So that it should not be moved forever, 6. You covered it with the deep as with a garment; The waters stood above the mountains. 7. At Your rebuke they fled; At the voice of Your thunder they hastened away. 8. They went up over the mountains; They went down into the valleys, To the place which You founded for them. 9. You have set a boundary that they may not pass over, That they may not return to cover the earth.

Scientists have hypothesized that when the canopy was broken up, the wind consequently began to form, allowing major evaporation and movements of air clouds. This would allow the water to recede from the earth's surface.

Now, the same Hebrew word *ruach* is used here to represent the wind, whereas it is used in Genesis 1:2 for God's spirit. Scholars agree there's some correlation, but we are not to make a fuss over the same usage; one means God's spirit, and the other is just wind. Again it's correct usage by the writer and just the same word translated or used in a different context.

There was also an instance in which the term for "God remembered" was used in narrating the time of Sodom when God remembered Abraham. As part of His action of remembering, He rescued Lot from the destruction. It is worth noting that when God sent His Son into the world, He did it in remembrance of His mercy as stated in Luke 1:54.

Luke 1:54 He has helped His servant Israel, In remembrance of His mercy.

Also, when the dying thief asked Jesus to remember him, he was asking that He take a decisive action on his behalf stated in Luke 23:42.

Luke 23:42. Then he said to Jesus, "Lord, remember me when You come into Your kingdom."

Maybe, one of the most effective prayers we could pray would be for the Lord to remember us by showing us mercy, seeing what we are reminded in James 2:13.

James 2:13. For judgment is without mercy to the one who has shown no mercy. Mercy triumphs over judgment.

Remember that God is merciful, but His judgement is just and timely.

The water receded from the face of the earth, and the situation returned to almost normal in Genesis 8:3.

Genesis 8:3. And the waters receded continually from the earth. At the end of the hundred and fifty days the waters decreased.

This is only after 150 days and after the water settled into new geological formations. The Bible mentions that on the seventeenth day the ark settled on top of Mt. Ararat. On the border of Armenia and Turkey stands a solitary mountain with a height of around 17,000 feet called Mt. Ararat. There are reported accounts that explorers have spotted from 14,000 feet something that resembles the ark. Historians have reported that pieces of wood from a boat were recovered from the site that could date between 1000 to 5000 years old.

There are many other sightings of the historical ark throughout the ages dating back as far as 275 BC. History suggests that people have found pieces of the ark and fashioned jewelry and other forms of keepsakes from them. We are not exactly sure what is up there and its true historical significance.

The biblical account of the "mountains" suggests that it is plural not singular. In addition, we will find in a much later chapter that Noah's sons journeyed from the east to reach the land of Shinar, whereas modern Ararat is to the north of Shinar. We must also accept that the naming of the mountain of Ararat is a recent event, where the "mountains of Ararat" denoted a large region north of the upper Mesopotamian Valley. In addition, we should note that Ararat is not the biblical name for the mountains but rather the name of the country in which the mountains were located.

Jeremiah 51:27. Set up a banner in the land, Blow the trumpet among the nations! Prepare the nations against her, Call the kingdoms together against her: Ararat, Minni, and Ashkenaz. Appoint a general against her; Cause the horses to come up like the bristling locusts.

Theologians believe that Ararat was another name for the ancient kingdom of Urartu, located in what is now the eastern part of turkey. That being said, here are some historical accounts written concerning the whereabouts of the ark.

In 275 BC Berosus, a Babylonian historian, wrote, "But of this ship that grounded in Armenia some part still remains in the mountains… and some get pitch from the ship by scraping it off."

Around AD 75, Josephus said the locals collected relics from the ark and showed them off to his own day. He also said all the ancient historians he knew of wrote about the ark.

In AD 180, Theophilus of Antioch wrote, "The remains, of the ark, are to this day to be seen... in the mountains."

An elderly Armenian man in America reported that as a boy, he visited the ark with his father and three atheistic scientists in 1856. Their goal was to disprove the ark's existence, but they found it and became so enraged they tried to destroy it. They could not, because it was too big and had petrified. In 1918, one of those atheistic scientists, who was British, admitted on his deathbed that the whole story was true.

Although physical proof could be helpful, our faith should never be solely dependent upon it rather the message of the great flood and the rescue effort through the ark as provided by God. This should not shake anyone's belief in the scripture as a reliable account on historic global flood. Rather, the flood's impact on the earth through geologic restructuring provides proof enough that there was a major catastrophe.

Psalms 119:160. The entirety of Your word is truth, And every one of Your righteous judgments endures forever.

Then Noah waited 40 days after the ark came to rest on the mountains of Ararat.

Genesis 8:6. So it came to pass, at the end of forty days, that Noah opened the window of the ark which he had made.

When Noah first opened the window, he must have exhaled a deep breath of relief. First, he sent out a raven to see if the waters of the flood had subsided. It scoured to and fro looking for dry land and didn't return. Perhaps this could've been because the raven is carnivorous and would feed off of dead carcasses.

Genesis 8:7. Then he sent out a raven, which kept going to and fro until the waters had dried up from the earth.

It seems to make sense that Noah would send the raven first just to see the condition of the waters and how they had subsided, giving credence to the historical accuracy of the Bible.

He then sent out a dove, the purpose perhaps for Noah being to get an indication of whether or not there was any vegetation. It didn't find any plant life; therefore the dove returned to the ark.

Genesis 8:8. He also sent out from himself a dove, to see if the waters had receded from the face of the ground. 9. But the dove found no resting place for the sole of her foot, and she returned into the ark to him, for the waters were on the face of the whole earth. So he put out his hand and took her, and drew her into the ark to himself.

Noah had a special relationship with his doves; the Bible mentions that the dove landed on his hand and he brought her back into the ark. The second time, however, the dove brought a freshly plucked olive leaf.

Genesis 8:10. And he waited yet another seven days, and again he sent the dove out from the ark. 11. Then the dove came to him in the evening, and behold, a freshly plucked olive leaf was in her mouth; and Noah knew that the waters had receded from the earth.

It is worthy to note that this is what most of us use as a symbol of peace. This was not the message for Noah. In this historical account, it is God's message that His judgement has not yet ended on earth. It was the third seventh-day dove that Noah sent out which did not return that indicated that God's judgement had ended and the earth had been restored. The absent dove should have been the symbol of peace, because that is when the earth was renewed again.

Genesis 8:12. So he waited yet another seven days and sent out the dove, which did not return again to him anymore.

This is the beginning of a new world, new hope, and God's restoration of mankind. It was in the first day of the first month during Noah's six hundredth year that the ark's covering was removed and the ground was dry. Then the second month proceeded, and God instructed Noah and his family to "go out of the ark".

Genesis 8:16. "Go out of the ark, you and your wife, and your sons and your sons' wives with you."

This marks the end of the antediluvian world that Noah had known. Noah would have to face a whole new world with only his wife and his three sons and their wives. Of course, this includes all the living creatures inside the ark; they would have the responsibility to repopulate the earth.

Noah obeyed God faithfully. God established a new covenant with Noah.

Genesis 8:20. Then Noah built an altar to the Lord, and took of every clean animal and of every clean bird, and offered burnt offerings on the altar. 21. And the Lord smelled a soothing aroma. Then the Lord said in His heart, "I will never again curse the ground for man's sake, although the imagination of man's heart is evil from his youth; nor will I again destroy every living thing as I have done. 22. While the earth remains, Seedtime and harvest, Cold and heat, winter and summer, And day and night Shall not cease."

This is the first reference to an altar within the Bible, and it's significant that the sacrifice is referred to as a burnt offering. This simply means that the offering was completely burned upon an altar. This is precisely the reason for bringing seven of every clean animal and bird: God wanted an offering of a "soothing aroma".

This is when God made his promise to Noah and to mankind.

Genesis 8:21. And the Lord smelled a soothing aroma. Then the Lord said in His heart, "I will never again curse the ground for man's sake, although the imagination of man's heart is evil from his youth; nor will I again destroy every living thing as I have done.

The solemnness of this simple worship service following the great catastrophe must've been awe inspiring. We witness a supreme act of worship and devotion to the Lord as the One to whom all of life belongs. It is the ultimate praise to God Almighty after a great deliverance experience. Today this would be similar to our praise and worship session that we do at home alone, with family, in our place of worship with extended family and friends, and even in a large gathering with people of God around the world. It should be our desire to worship God Almighty anytime in spirit and in truth wherever we are able to. Praise the Lord God Almighty who was, who is, and who is to come.

Genesis 8:22. "While the earth remains, Seedtime and harvest, Cold and heat, Winter and summer, And day and night Shall not cease."

God made another promise to mankind. He assured Noah and his descendants that the world would continue as it was; planting season—and the climate of each season—all would be restored and remain the same. God received Noah's sacrifice as an act of worship with openness.

Some catastrophist scientists believe that the flood was the cataclysm that tilted the earth 23.5 degrees on its axis, giving us our four seasons. This explains the invention of four seasons (which some would call climate changes). Then He promised He would never again smite every living thing, “as I have done”.

It is worthy to note that this manner of speaking was used by Paul, for example when he described the gifts of the Christians at Philippi as being an odor of sweet smell, a sacrifice acceptable, well pleasing to God.

Philippians 4:18. Indeed I have all and abound. I am full, having received from Epaphroditus the things sent from you, a sweet-smelling aroma, an acceptable sacrifice, well pleasing to God.

Ephesians 5:2. And walk in love, as Christ also has loved us and given Himself for us, an offering and a sacrifice to God for a sweet-smelling aroma.

God didn’t make His promise to Noah because we would not fall into sin again. Rather, His reckoning would be in a different form of judgement. God is merciful but His judgement is inevitable. 2 Peter 3:10-13 foretold in what manner God will punish this sinful world.

2 Peter 3:10. But the day of the Lord will come as a thief in the night, in which the heavens will pass away with a great noise, and the elements will melt with fervent heat; both the earth and the works that are in it will be burned up. 11. Therefore, since all these things will be dissolved, what manner of persons ought you to be in holy conduct and godliness, 12. looking for and hastening the coming of the day of God, because of which the heavens will be dissolved, being on fire, and the elements will melt with fervent heat? 13. Nevertheless we, according to His promise, look for new heavens and a new earth in which righteousness dwells.

Shining a light on the words "never again", God is showing us His willingness to be patient and long-suffering to those who commit sin and rebel against Him. Even though He knows that our hearts have a tendency toward evil, He will continue to keep the universe in order or orderly, allowing the sun to shine and the rain to fall on both good and bad people. God seems to emphasize His plan not for destruction, but rather for redemption to save humankind. It is worthy to note that this is going to be the central message of the rest of the Bible.

Although there is an enormous amount of evidence that points to the global flood, there are those that still cling to the local nature or non-existence of that flood. Why is this? Simple; they do not want to know that God's judgement is coming.

What God did to destroy sinners in the antediluvian period He will do again in the future. The second half of the book of Revelation will provide details of God's coming judgement. But there is an "ark of safety" for us today and His name is Jesus Christ, the only Son of God.

Even to those unbelievers, the scriptures provide a historical narrative that is confirmed by writers even outside of Genesis account. Almost every book of the Bible makes some form of mention or reference to the book of Genesis. Even the New Testament books have many references to Genesis and its concepts. Moreover, if Jesus believed that the historical account of Genesis as stated in Mark 10:6 is accurate, then it is proof enough that Genesis is a true historical account.

Mark 10:6. But from the beginning of the creation, God "made them male and female."

Today we rest on the truth that Jesus is the door to our ark of safety. If you would turn from sin and trust in God's plan of salvation by giving your life to Him, you will be saved. God will remember you like He remembered Noah.

Heavenly Father, we rest in your hope of salvation through Jesus Christ, your only Son. We are grateful that you remembered Noah, thereby continuing your redemption plan. We thank you for giving us understanding of why you caused the global flood to occur and how we can be rescued from your coming judgement. We believe that through Jesus, we have forgiveness of sins and an eternal hope for salvation. We pray all this in Jesus' name, amen.

CHAPTER 9
THE BEGINNING OF COVENANTS

Bob was in a terrible motorcycle accident and his legs weren't in great shape, to say the least. After a couple of weeks of therapy, it soon became clear to the doctor that they were just pushing off the inevitable. Due, however, to Bob's frail condition, the doctor was afraid to give him the bad news. Instead, he gave the sorry job to Bob's wife of 40 years, hoping that she would know how to break the bad news to him ever so slowly and gently.

Eva: "Honey, I've got good news and bad news; which one would you like to hear first?"

Bob, always in a morbid state, responded in his usual grumpy voice: "What do I care? Just give me the bad news!"

Eva: "Well dear, I hate to have to tell you this, but it seems like your legs are going to have to be taken off."

Bob, barely able to hold his voice from cracking, croaked out, "Eva, what's the good news?"

Eva: "The good news is that that the gardener that was in here just before said he may be interested in buying your shoes from you."

The chapter begins with God blessing Noah and his sons and telling them be fruitful and multiply. This announcement upon Noah and his family affirms the original blessing given earlier to the human family in Genesis 1:28.

Genesis 1:28. Then God blessed them, and God said to them, "Be fruitful and multiply; fill the earth and subdue it; have dominion over the fish of the sea, over the birds of the air, and over every living thing that moves on the earth."

The beginning of new life for Noah and his family is simple, but its simplicity is coupled with instruction to have order and purpose. God's instruction was also simple: populate the earth. If one were to ask the question, "What is the meaning of life?" the short answer is, "Be fruitful and multiply; fill the earth."

This is still true today; God wants us to fill this earth with Christian children. We need to perpetuate life with children that will advance the Christian world view. To those who still debate whether abortion is in line with the Christian worldview, short answer is no. If Genesis is not sufficient proof that God views life as sacred, then Psalms may offer us added help.

Psalms 127:3. Behold, children are a heritage from the Lord, The fruit of the womb is a reward.

Psalms 139:13. For You formed my inward parts; You covered me in my mother's womb. 14. I will praise You, for I am fearfully and wonderfully made; Marvelous are Your works, And that my soul knows very well. 15. My frame was not hidden from You, When I was made in secret, And skillfully wrought in the lowest parts of the earth. 16. Your eyes saw my substance, being yet unformed. And in Your book they all were written, The days fashioned for me, When as yet there were none of them.

The Bible is very clear on the sanctity of human life; born or unborn, it is sacred. Beyond Genesis, Moses laid out the laws precisely on this subject. If the unborn is killed within the mother's womb, then it is murder and the punishment will fit the crime.

Exodus 21:22. If men fight, and hurt a woman with child, so that she gives birth prematurely, yet no harm follows, he shall surely be punished accordingly as the woman's husband imposes on him; and he shall pay as the judges determine. 23. But if any harm follows, then you shall give life for life, 24. eye for eye, tooth for tooth, hand for hand, foot for foot, 25. burn for burn, wound for wound, stripe for stripe.

Although manslaughter is still charged in many US states if a child in the womb is murdered, some states allow the legal removal of "tissue" in the form of abortion because of the 1973 Supreme Court decision of Roe vs. Wade. The justification was that the woman's right to privacy overrides the unborn child's right to life. Since that dark day on January 22, 1973, over sixty million American babies have been murdered through abortion. God's judgement will be upon us for this atrocity.

However, Noah heeded God's command and began to repopulate the earth, forming a society. This basic instruction is the model of society. Society will form a government. We will talk more about human government later in the chapter. For now, just know this is a brand-new world and God wants it filled with people who will walk according to His instructions. This self-governing authority is given not only to Noah and his family but to us today. God wants us to perpetuate life so that the earth will be filled with God-loving and caring people who will give God the praise and glory.

Additionally, Noah and his family were given control over the animals, the fish and the birds. This is another key ingredient to the forming of human society. Dominion over animals allows humans to use the animal kingdom for the benefit of mankind to populate the earth. Consider this: in a world in which humans are inferior to animals the result is extinction of humans. Humans are the crowning of all life on earth; we are not animals and do not belong to the animal kind as suggested by some scientific books.

Genesis 9:2. And the fear of you and the dread of you shall be on every beast of the earth, on every bird of the air, on all that move on the earth, and on all the fish of the sea. They are given into your hand.

According to science of zoology, when animals come in contact with man, for the most part, animals are afraid and will avoid confrontation. Even a large beast such as an elephant will run away from humans unless cornered or provoked. If you threaten their young or get in their space, they will fight back, but this is only for self-preservation. Their nature is to avoid humans and run away.

God says "the fear of you shall be on every beast." This makes sense in the perspective of how the animal kingdom reproduces faster and more often than humanity. The animal kingdom could easily overrun humans by their rapid growth, causing overpopulation. The next idea that the Bible introduces to mankind helps control the animal population, hunting and killing them for consumption.

Here God adds something new to the human scene. Up until now everyone has been solely vegetarian (Genesis 1:29-30), but permission is now given by God to eat the meat of animals and birds. This helps solve for the lack of dry land to farm at that time.

Genesis 9:3. Every moving thing that lives shall be food for you. I have given you all things, even as the green herbs. 4. But you shall not eat flesh with its life, that is, its blood. 5. Surely for your lifeblood I will demand a reckoning; from the hand of every beast I will require it, and from the hand of man. From the hand of every man's brother I will require the life of man.

From omnivores to carnivores, we have evolved by God's direction. God's command was to eat animals and plants. But God cautioned us to avoid the blood of those animals. The reason is given that life is in the blood, and life belongs only to God.

From Adam to Seth and down to Noah, the dietary habit was to eat plants. However, the structure of your mouth and teeth indicates a design to tear and chew on meat product. There are those who hold a belief that the Bible preaches holiness that equates with being a vegetarian. Well, this scripture proves otherwise. We can argue the benefits for being vegetarians against not being vegetarians, with sound reasoning for both. Still, it is the Bible that is the authority on our diet.

However, God did forbid us to eat blood. Not only in Genesis, but other later books of the Bible forbid the eating of the blood.

Deuteronomy 12:23. Only be sure that you do not eat the blood, for the blood is the life; you may not eat the life with the meat.

This means we should not eat live animals. Our body doesn't have the antibodies to fend off the bacteria that are present in living animal blood. Further in the Bible, the Leviticus writer tells us that the life of the flesh is in the blood, and with the blood, you will make atonement.

Leviticus 17:11. For the life of the flesh is in the blood, and I have given it to you upon the altar to make atonement for your souls; for it is the blood that makes atonement for the soul.'

Therefore, it is more than just for our health; it is for the atonement of our sins. It is by the blood of Jesus that we will make our atonement. There is power in the blood of Jesus.

We can pray over what food we eat, but it is what comes out of our mouth we must guard against.

Mark 7:15. There is nothing that enters a man from outside which can defile him; but the things which come out of him, those are the things that defile a man.

Changes of dietary habits occurred many times, even in the New Testament. It is worthwhile to note the conversation between God and Peter that begins in Acts 10:9.

Acts 10:9. The next day, as they went on their journey and drew near the city, Peter went up on the housetop to pray, about the sixth hour. 10. Then he became very hungry and wanted to eat; but while they made ready, he fell into a trance 11. and saw heaven opened and an object like a great sheet bound at the four corners, descending to him and let down to the earth. 12. In it were all kinds of four-footed animals of the earth, wild beasts, creeping things, and birds of the air. 13. And a voice came to him, "Rise, Peter; kill and eat." 14. But Peter said, "Not so, Lord! For I have never eaten anything common or unclean." 15. And a voice spoke to him again the second time, "What God has cleansed you must not call common." 16. This was done three times. And the object was taken up into heaven again.

The difficulty for Peter shown in this conversation is that it seems he was hearing God speaking against his belief, which he held because of his lack of understanding of the law and intent of the law. God's repeated instruction to Peter convinced him to accept that what God has blessed, and that it should never be called unclean or common.

When we pray and bless the food we eat, God's blessing is upon it. Therefore, the food has become clean and safe to eat.

God states the sacredness of human life by forbidding a person to take the life of another person; of course, with this warning he gives us the consequences of doing so.

Genesis 9:6. Whoever sheds man's blood, By man his blood shall be shed; For in the image of God He made man.

Moses wrote an elaboration of God's command in Genesis. In Exodus 21:12-26 he gives a specific account about how to follow the law of preservation of human life.

Exodus 21:12. He who strikes a man so that he dies shall surely be put to death. 13. However, if he did not lie in wait, but God delivered him into his hand, then I will appoint for you a place where he may flee. 14. But if a man acts with premeditation against his neighbor, to kill him by treachery, you shall take him from My altar, that he may die. 15. And he who strikes his father or his mother shall surely be put to death. 16. He who kidnaps a man and sells him, or if he is found in his hand, shall surely be put to death. 17. And he who curses his father or his mother shall surely be put to death. 18. If men contend with each other, and one strikes the other with a stone or with his fist, and he does not die but is confined to his bed, 19. if he rises again and walks about outside with his staff, then he who struck him shall be acquitted. He shall only pay for the loss of his time, and shall provide for him to be thoroughly healed. 20. And if a man beats his male or female servant with a rod, so that he dies under his hand, he shall surely be punished. 21. Notwithstanding, if he remains alive a day or two, he shall not be punished; for he is his property. 22. If men fight, and hurt a woman with child, so that she gives birth prematurely, yet no harm follows, he shall surely be punished accordingly as the woman's husband imposes on him; and he shall pay as the judges determine. 23. But if any harm follows, then you shall give life for life, 24. eye for eye, tooth for tooth, hand for hand, foot for foot, 25. burn for burn, wound for wound, stripe for stripe. 26. If a man strikes the eye of his male or female servant, and destroys it, he shall let him go free for the sake of his eye. 27. And if he knocks out the tooth of his male or female servant, he shall let him go free for the sake of his tooth.

After God placed a fear of man into animals, He emphasized the fear of God to man. Perhaps the most productive instruction that God handed down to man is the preservation of life. Beginning with Cain's horrific act toward his brother and then Lamech killing a young man, the antediluvian world was filled with violence and death. The world seems to value human life very little.

The specific guidance listed in Exodus is to subdue the violent tendency of human society. This example within human history gives us an affirmation that human life is sacred because we're created in the image of God, *Imago Dei*. Life is a precious gift from God, and only He can take life, and for someone to take a life is to usurp God's control over His creation. God states the sacredness of human life by forbidding a person to take a life of another person

Of course, with this warning He gives us the consequences of doing so. This is the foundation for growth of human society. This is not an old concept, only listed in the Old Testament. Paul affirms this notion in the New Testament also.

Romans 13:1. Let every soul be subject to the governing authorities. For there is no authority except from God, and the authorities that exist are appointed by God. 2. Therefore whoever resists the authority resists the ordinance of God, and those who resist will bring judgment on themselves. 3. For rulers are not a terror to good works, but to evil. Do you want to be unafraid of the authority? Do what is good, and you will have praise from the same. 4. For he is God's minister to you for good. But if you do evil, be afraid; for he does not bear the sword in vain; for he is God's minister, an avenger to execute wrath on him who practices evil. 5. Therefore you must be subject, not only because of wrath but also for conscience' sake. 6. For because of this you also pay taxes, for they are God's ministers attending continually to this very thing. 7. Render therefore to all their due: taxes to whom taxes are due, customs to whom customs, fear to whom fear, honor to whom honor. 8. Owe no one anything except to love one another, for he who loves another has fulfilled the law. 9. For the commandments, "You shall not commit adultery," "You shall not murder," "You shall not steal," "You shall not bear false witness," "You shall not covet," and if there is any other commandment, are all summed up in this saying, namely, "You shall love your neighbor as yourself." 10. Love does no harm to a neighbor; therefore love is the fulfillment of the law.

In Romans 13:1-10, God informs of the basis of human government. It states that God gives the authority to uphold the law and commands us to follow it as a faithful participant of our society. God's instruction is for us to submit to human government as to His divine authority when it comes to preservation of human life.

A dictionary definition of government is "the political direction and control exercised over the actions of the members, citizens, or inhabitants of communities, societies, and states". This authority is given by God with the exercise of capital punishment. If one disagrees with government, their punishment may ensue, and the final punishment could be of grave consequence. For those who are in opposition to this decree by God, then my advice would be not to commit such offense, but ensure that no grave result will visit you.

The Bible is the authority for the formation of human laws, and God instructs us to obey all of His laws. It is only when human laws conflict with God's laws that we are to resist government.

Through these instructions and decrees handed down by God, He is introducing a new bond, a sort of cooperation between God and man. The scripture called this a covenant. Covenant is a binding promise or agreement; we sometimes refer to it as a contract.

Genesis 9:9. And as for Me, behold, I establish My covenant with you and with your descendants after you.

The idea of covenant which we find in the latter scriptures goes to the heart of the Bible. The word *beriyth* in Hebrew not only occurs about 286 times; the best explanation of the word is that it comes from the same root word *berit* which means "cutting" because pacts were made by passing between cut pieces of flesh of the victim of an animal sacrifice. Most covenants made in the ancient days involved some form of visible representation of an invisible agreement between two or more parties.

This is why God used the rainbow as visible representation of His promise not to ever destroy humanity with water. It is true that no one had ever seen a rainbow in antediluvian world. From a scientific perspective, this makes sense because a rainbow comes sunshine and downpour of water in the atmosphere; this wasn't the condition before the flood. It had never rained. The simple phenomenon of rain droplets refracting sunlight displays an array of red, orange, yellow, green, blue, purple, and pink. It's the shape of a bow, which was normally used as a war sign; instead, God used it to show His peace with humankind.

We admire the rainbow as a happy connection with God, rather than anger of war. I have lived in the state of Hawaii, which uses the rainbow as a symbol; it has always meant happiness and peace. “Aloha” means love, and the rainbow state motto signifies the true meaning of love and happiness.

God’s promise not to ever repeat his destruction of people with water should comfort us; this is the covenant of God and man. The greatest covenant would later be manifested in the person of Jesus Christ dying on the cross and being resurrected on the third day, and He now has sat down at the right hand of the throne of God.

The idea is that covenant is a treaty or an agreement binding two parties together.

Let’s talk a little more about covenants. They fall into two categories and into two classes. There are unconditional and conditional covenants.

An unconditional covenant is unilateral and requires no responsive action from the other party. On the other hand, a conditional covenant is where two parties each require action from the other in order for the agreement to become valid.

In the Noahic unconditional covenant, as some Bible scholars would term it, God promises Noah that never again would He destroy the earth and people with water. God would make many more covenants with His people throughout the scriptures, both conditional and unconditional.

In addition, as mentioned earlier in this book, there are also covenants made between equal parties and between unequal parties. When a covenant was made between two equals, the obligations were equally binding on both parties. A good example of this kind of covenant was the one made between David and Jonathan.

1 Samuel 20:14. And you shall not only show me the kindness of the Lord while I still live, that I may not die; 15. but you shall not cut off your kindness from my house forever, no, not when the Lord has cut off every one of the enemies of David from the face of the earth." 16. So Jonathan made a covenant with the house of David, saying, "Let the Lord require it at the hand of David's enemies."

The second kind of covenant was unequal, between masters and their slaves or between rulers and their subjects. It was this kind of covenant that God made with Noah, a covenant not between equals, but offered by the greater to the lesser.

The covenant made with Noah in this part of the Bible is the second time this type is mentioned. The first was the conditional Edenic covenant, as theologians would phrase it; it was when God offered Adam all that the Garden had to eat except one tree, but Adam failed.

However, with Noah, God entered into a covenant that would span generations. Although, God made the covenant only with Noah, it benefited all of his descendants within, as we see in Genesis 9:9-11.

Genesis 9:9. "And as for Me, behold, I establish My covenant with you and with your descendants after you, 10. and with every living creature that is with you: the birds, the cattle, and every beast of the earth with you, of all that go out of the ark, every beast of the earth.

11. Thus I establish My covenant with you: Never again shall all flesh be cut off by the waters of the flood; never again shall there be a flood to destroy the earth."

This included not only human beings but every living creature. The covenant assured Noah and his descendants that there would never again be a flood that would wipe out all human life. This covenant designed perpetually, for generations. This seems to suggest that it is an everlasting one. The rainbow shows God's promise to humankind will never end.

God also reveals to us in the New Testament a promise of grace. This is the New Covenant referenced within John 1:17.

John 1:17. For the law was given through Moses, but grace and truth came through Jesus Christ.

After God created and revealed His marvelous covenant in the form of a rainbow, the writer introduces us to the sad part of this chapter. Noah sinned against God.

We read that Noah became a vineyard farmer. He was successful in producing wine. In the peak of his success, Noah drank wine in excess and one day was found sprawled out naked in his tent.

Genesis 9:21. Then he drank of the wine and was drunk, and became uncovered in his tent. 22. And Ham, the father of Canaan, saw the nakedness of his father, and told his two brothers outside.

It is no use to pretend that none of us sin, because we all fall short of the glory of God. Nevertheless, it is disheartening to know that Noah fell into the sin of drunkenness. It is worth noting that Noah walked with God for hundreds of years and was redeemed for his faithfulness. But he fell to the temptation of overindulgence in wine. It does remind us that the flood, while being a judgement for sinfulness, didn't necessarily eradicate sin.

Ephesians 5:18. And do not be drunk with wine, in which is dissipation; but be filled with the Spirit.

Paul reminds us to not be drunk with wine but filled with the Spirit. Having grown up with an alcoholic father, I have witnessed the devastating effect of alcohol on man's physical and spiritual wellbeing. Don't be deceived by alcohol; it is not wise to consume it.

Proverbs 20:1. Wine is a mocker, Strong drink is a brawler, and whoever is led astray by it is not wise.

One cannot be wise and be addicted to alcohol. In this instance, God's blessing of food and drink has become Noah's stumbling block. Then, we discover when Ham found his father in a drunken state, rather than covering him up, he mocked him and went and told his brothers, Shem and Japheth.

Proverbs 20:20. Whoever curses his father or his mother, His lamp will be put out in deep darkness.

In our culture, media has desensitized us to nakedness; we may not think it is a big deal. The Bible points out this act of disrespect to a father from his son is a sign of disrespect against God's law. As we will see later, in Leviticus 18, God views Ham's act towards his father as a punishable offense.

Leviticus 18:7. The nakedness of your father or the nakedness of your mother you shall not uncover. She is your mother; you shall not uncover her nakedness.

Therefore, it is justifiable that Noah cursed Canaan, Ham's descendants. Ham's offense of attempting to usurp his father's authority by belittling his condition to others is a punishable offense in their custom. Noah's cursed shows that he is trying to reciprocate Ham's disrespect of him by foretelling how Ham's next generation would do the same. Ham's sons would dishonor him as he dishonored his father, Noah. This prophecy would come to fruition, as we see in the future that Israel would defeat the Canaanites and live in their land.

Leviticus 24:20. ...fracture for fracture, eye for eye, tooth for tooth;

As Ham has caused a form of disfigurement of a man, so shall it be done to him; this is the basis of Noah's curse of Ham.

The two brothers did their father a favor by covering his shame, as they walk backward to avoid seeing their father's nakedness in Genesis 9:23.

Genesis 9:23. But Shem and Japheth took a garment, laid it on both their shoulders, and went backward and covered the nakedness of their father. Their faces were turned away, and they did not see their father's nakedness.

This display of proper respect for elders is the bedrock of Hebrew society. Shem and Japheth showed respect for their father in spite of their father's sinful condition.

Many in the past have taken Noah's act in the above verse out of the context of the meaning of this scripture. The Bible does state that Noah awoke from his wine and began to curse Canaan because of Ham's action. However, this was a curse of that particular tribe, and not meant to suggest slavery was justifiable for all of Canaan's descendants. Some have used this scripture to permit slavery of African people because of the curse, but this is the wrong idea and is simply wrong. Some who have accepted this skewed idea did so because Ham's descendants were thought by some to have settled in Africa. For slavers and early Christians teaching to accept slavery as a biblical concept was a gross misreading of the scriptures and of God's will within the Bible.

In the context of the scripture, God permitted the descendants of Shem (the Hebrews) and the descendants of Japheth (possibly the Philistines) to subjugate the Canaanites. This interpretation would be used as a reason for the conquest of Canaan by the Hebrews after the exodus, and it suggests that God allowed this to happen because of the moral corruption of the Canaanites and their ancestors.

Deuteronomy 9:4. Do not think in your heart, after the Lord your God has cast them out before you, saying, "Because of my righteousness the Lord has brought me in to possess this land"; but it is because of the wickedness of these nations that the Lord is driving them out from before you.

We see that accounts of Noah's son's descendants come into view within the later verses. God favored Shem and his descendants to fulfill God's role in His plan of redemption. Shem is known as Shemites, from which we get the word Semites today. We will later see in the scriptures that Shem's generation would include Abram (who later become Abraham).

It is from Abraham that the nation of Israel would emerge, and hence the deliverer that would fulfill the prophecy of Genesis 3:15. Jesus, the Messiah, would crush the head of the serpent.

Dear Heavenly Father, thank you for the clarity of the scripture. It is our prayer that you continue to show your plan of salvation through your son Jesus Christ, our Lord. Your revelation of the covenant you made with Noah to not destroy this world and everything in it with water, bringing us your symbol of that promise as a rainbow, assures us and gives us hope. We pray for your blessing, and we praise you in the name of Jesus, amen.

CHAPTER 10
THE BEGINNING OF NATIONS

Nagging wife: Honey, I have some good news and some bad news.

Husband: Just tell me, honey.

Nagging wife: I'm losing my voice.

Husband: And what's the bad news?

This primeval history will be coming to a conclusion; Genesis helps us trace humanity back to the origins. The Bible has the oldest ethnological list in history. "Ethnological" comes from the word "ethnology", which means a study of the characteristics of various people and the differences and relationships between them.

Within this chapter, we will see the Hebrews preserving their genealogies and records of ancestors; experts say that these are the oldest preserved genealogies. By now, we know that everyone on Earth is a direct descendant of Noah; we just have to decide which of the three sons we descended from in our lineage.

The Hebrews were the only people in antiquity who believed in their hearts that all the nations of the earth had a common origin and Creator. It is worth noting that the genealogical list includes the names of 70 leaders of tribes, individuals who became heads of nations or people groups. This number is significant for the Hebrew people; it is a representation of the concept of wholeness or completion.

The sons of Noah were eventually divided by language, geography, characteristics, and their cultures. It is important to point out that the Bible's message is that we are all one race and one people. If we can transcend above any notion that the human race is fundamentally diverse, then we can begin to understand the fullness of God's purpose in creation.

Genesis 10:1. Now this is the genealogy of the sons of Noah: Shem, Ham, and Japheth. And sons were born to them after the flood.

The reading of this chapter becomes challenging because there are lots of names to follow.

It is interesting how the Bible lists the names in the first verse from youngest to oldest (Shem, Ham, and Japheth); but later the names are listed on the reverse order (Japheth, Ham, and Shem). It is not known if this is of any significance; it is just interesting to note. We do know that the youngest is Shem, then Ham, followed by Japheth.

We will follow the family line of each son, but it is worth noting that Shem's line is the most important to the scripture because this will lead us to Abraham and to Jesus Christ our Lord.

Among the Hebrews, the preserving of genealogical records of ancestors is a carefully preserved tradition. The purpose behind the writings is to trace the ancestry of Abraham back to Adam. Primeval history gives us a glimpse of how all nations have a common origin and share in the blessing and protection of the common Creator.

Now we see Genesis as more than just a book of beginnings; it is also a book of blessings. God has blessed Noah's sons to make them become fathers of all existing nations.

We find that from Japheth come fourteen nations. Japheth was prophesied to mean "to enlarge" as the name suggests. It is known that Japheth's descendants migrated and settled in Europe, and they're known as the Indo-European people with its languages. We know from history that Japheth's descendants have often been classified as barbaric and uncivilized.

Shem's descendants helped to enlighten them and help humanity become more godly, and they were blessed as their territory grew, reaching out to the continent of Africa, Asia, and even America.

We notice that Japheth had seven sons and seven grandsons, at least, as far as listed in the Bible.

Genesis 10:2. The sons of Japheth were Gomer, Magog, Madai, Javan, Tubal, Meshech, and Tiras. 3. The sons of Gomer were Ashkenaz, Riphath, and Togarmah. 4. The sons of Javan were Elishah, Tarshish, Kittim, and Dodanim. 5. From these the coastland peoples of the Gentiles were separated into their lands, everyone according to his language, according to their families, into their nations.

Historical accounts list the lineage of Gomer, whose offspring settled and became known as the ancient Cimmerians and Scythians in Asia Minor. They continued to expand into eastern and central Europe, finally reaching northern Europe. We can also learn about Gomerland, more familiar to us as it became known as Cumberland of the Celts, peoples who settled as far north as northern Britain and beyond. We know that these groups of people migrated to Scotland, Ireland, and Wales.

History tells us that the Magog lineage brought us the ancient Russians, Slavs, Bulgarians, Bohemians, Poles, and Croats. Ancient writings suggest that the wall of China was also known as the wall of Magog because it was to protect the ancient Chinese cities from the Magogites. This history is mentioned by Herodotus in 5 BC, and Josephus in 1 AD about these people.

Then we have Madai, who settled in Persia, a great empire in the Middle East that blankets areas such as Iran, Afghanistan, and the Kurdish people. We know now that since the breakup of the Persian empires, newer countries such as Iran and Iraq have been fighting each other. This is due to the fact that Iraq was settled by the Shemites—Arabic people—while the neighboring Iranians trace their roots to Japhethites (or Persians). It goes further back than just the infighting within the Islamic faith; the root goes all the way to the two sons of Noah.

The other son of Japheth is Javan or Yevon, from whom we got the Greeks, and eventually they settled in Italy and became Romans. The Tubals and descendants of Meshech settled in the eastern Europe and northeast of the Black Sea, which we know now as Russia. We can trace the name of Meshech and Tubal to two Russian cities known as Moscow, near Muskva River, and Tubalksk, near the Tubal River.

According to Josephus, Tiras was a father of the Eutruscan races that settled the far eastern coast of Aegean Sea of Asia Minor. That completes the first lineage of Japheth and his sons.

Ethnologists and linguists know that there is a language base called the Indo-European, as linguists trace the origin of our language to the ancient Indian Sanskrit. They know that the origins of peoples who settled in Europe have their roots in Iran, India, and central Asia, being the sons of Japheth.

Genesis 10:6. The sons of Ham were Cush, Mizraim, Put, and Canaan.

The Bible now begins to give us the lineage of Ham. Historians put his descendants in the group of people who migrated to southwest Mesopotamia, Egypt, and the rest of northern and eastern Africa. Cush settled in ancient Ethiopia.

Jeremiah 13:23. Can the Ethiopian change his skin or the leopard its spots? Then may you also do good who are accustomed to do evil.

The Cushite is described here as having a distinct skin color. *Mizraim* is the ancient name used by the Hebrews to refer to Egypt; it means "mound" or "fortress". *Put* was a reference to Libya. This brings us to the most important of Ham's sons, who is Canaan.

Genesis 9:25. Then he said: "Cursed be Canaan; a servant of servants he shall be to his brethren."

Let's go back a little to the previous chapter and revisit the scripture. History's dark past puts this scripture into the focus for the justification of slavery in the 1800's, as mentioned before. This misinterpretation of the scripture went along with the capturing and enslaving of tribes from Africa (as Ham is the father of the African peoples), falsely imparting to them the curse upon Canaan.

However, this particular one of Ham's sons settled in ancient Israel and Palestine, being known as the Canaanite peoples. This is the reason behind why Israel needed to conquer the land of the Canaanite.

Genesis 10:15. Canaan begot Sidon his firstborn, and Heth; 16. the Jebusite, the Amorite, and the Girgashite; 17. the Hivite, the Arkite, and the Sinite; 18. the Arvadite, the Zemarite, and the Hamathite. Afterward the families of the Canaanites were dispersed. 19. And the border of the Canaanites was from Sidon as you go toward Gerar, as far as Gaza; then as you go toward Sodom, Gomorrah, Admah, and Zeboiim, as far as Lasha. 20. These were the sons of Ham, according to their families, according to their languages, in their lands and in their nations

The children of Israel were told to conquer the Gurgashite, Hivite, Hittite, Jebusite—in other words, all the Canaanite people.

Then we move ahead, noting Cush's son Havilah, who became the father of the people of Arabia. However, the most famous of Cush's sons is Nimrod, "a mighty hunter before the Lord" (Genesis 10:9). Nimrod, according to ancient historians, was the first king of Babylon known as Sargon Agade. In ancient times, kings had many names; he has commonly been called Sargon the First. Nimrod established his kingdom in Babylon in the Mesopotamian river valley, and he was also a ruler of Nineveh, the city he built in Assyria.

Nimrod's carving out of an empire for himself was evidently seen as a violation of God's purpose of peace and coexistence among the nations. Nimrod became the father of the ancient enemies of the Hebrew people, because Assyria and Babylonia were the nations that exiled the Jews from their homeland. This occurred from 586 BC to 722 BC. Genesis 10:11 makes reference some sites and people, but historians are still debating the exact locations of some of the real places.

Genesis 10:11. From that land he went to Assyria and built Nineveh, Rehoboth Ir, Calah....

We do recognize some of the names mentioned in later verses, such as the Philistines, descendants of Casluhim, son of Mizraim, and the cities of Sodom and Gomorrah (Canaanites).

Some historians want to include the Mongol tribes and the Native Americans as well as the South Islanders under the Hamitic descendants. Although further genealogies could shed more light on the Hamites, this is not an ethnology study.

Genesis 10:22. The sons of Shem were Elam, Asshur, Arphaxad, Lud, and Aram.

The last of Noah's sons, Shem gave us the Shemites, which is where God set up the lineage of the Messiah, Jesus of Nazareth. We know the redemptive nature of the biblical theme focuses on God's people.

"The father of all the children of Eber" (Genesis 10:21) denotes that the Hebrew people derived from *Eberew*, "people of Eber". Eber was Shem's great grandson and father of many who came after him. In later chapters of Genesis, we will see the appearance of Elam (the Elamites), Asshur (Assyria), and Aram (Aramean).

The prophet Daniel spoke an Aramean language called Aramaic while he was in captivity in Babylonia. It remained the prominent language of that time until Alexander the Great conquered the Babylonians and Greek became the dominant global language.

The overarching message of this chapter is that God is the history maker. He is in control of the history of the world and the origin of humanity. The Great Flood was central to the beginning of human history, and through the lineage of Noah's sons we have the great civilization and the different ethnicities and cultures known today. Although the lifespan of humans shrank from 900 years to 120 years due to the effects of sin, humans continued to flourish, and perpetual life continues throughout the world.

Through Shem, God chose to continue His redemptive plan and set a timeline that would fulfill His real salvation of humankind, setting a path for eternal fellowship with Him through His Son and our Savior, Jesus Christ.

Heavenly Father, you are the creator of nations. We are in awe when we see your mighty hand creating all that is in this world. The history of humanity is that you have redeemed us from the sin we were engaged in. Through your Son Jesus Christ, you have made us heirs to your heavenly kingdom. We pray all this in your name, Jesus, amen.

CHAPTER 11
THE TOWER OF CONFUSION

After coming down from Mt. Sinai, Moses spoke to the children of Israel.

Moses: I have some good news and bad news.

People: Tell us the good news first.

Moses: I have negotiated down to only 10 commandments from God.

Moses: And the bad news is, adultery stays!

The beginning of chapter eleven starts with the writer pointing out that the earth had one language and one speech. The original intent of the Lord is for people to be able to communicate and work together to build His kingdom on earth.

Matthew 6:10. Your kingdom come. Your will be done On earth as it is in heaven.

The human race was united in mind, spirit, and body. The Lord commanded Noah and his sons to populate and fill the earth.

Genesis 9:1. So God blessed Noah and his sons, and said to them: "Be fruitful and multiply, and fill the earth."

However, the people of this time decided to congregate in the east, near a land called Shinar, which was later known to be Babylon. With only 235 words and nine verses, we begin with the story of the tower of Babel, in Hebrew *balal* which means to "confuse" or "confound".

Next, we have a clear picture of the building of a city in the land of Shinar (modern-day Iraq), where people teamed up together in an arrogant rebellion against God. The people had a plan to build a tower that would reach up to heaven. The plain in the land of Shinar refers to the entire Mesopotamian valley; it was the broad expanse between the Tigris and the Euphrates rivers.

Genesis 11:4. And they said, "Come, let us build ourselves a city, and a tower whose top is in the heavens; let us make a name for ourselves, lest we be scattered abroad over the face of the whole earth."

The scripture tells us that they were doing this to "make a name for ourselves". In other words, the boastful pride of life.

1 John 2:16. For all that is in the world—the lust of the flesh, the lust of the eyes, and the pride of life—is not of the Father but is of the world.

The writer explains to us how the motive for their action was boastful pride of life; they wanted to make a name for themselves and to dictate their own movements and actions. They did not want to be scattered, and they wanted to take control of their own destiny instead of relying on God.

It is worth noting that the process of brickmaking was introduced within the scripture. Bricks are known as one of the oldest building materials found in history. Brickmaking stretches from Neolithic China around 4400 BC at Chengtoushan to southern Turkey at the site of an ancient settlement near Jericho around 5000 BC.

Today we can see traces of remains of a somewhat similar temple structure called the ziggurat. Archaeologists have uncovered this ancient ziggurat structure in Mesopotamia. A ziggurat was built to honor the main god of the city. The tradition of building a ziggurat was started by the Sumerians, but other civilizations of Mesopotamia such as the Akkadians, the Babylonians, and the Assyrians also built ziggurats. It was a rectangular stepped tower, sometimes surmounted by a temple. It was used essentially to worship the Zodiac, and they climbed to the center to be able to worship. They looked to the stars to worship the stars of heaven.

A ziggurat was first attested in the late 3rd millennium BC and probably inspired the biblical story of the tower of Babel. Instead of looking to God, they worshipped God's creation, the stars in heaven. This was the beginning of secular humanism and false religion based on astrology—not to be confused with astronomy. (Astronomy is the branch of science which deals with celestial objects, space, and the physical universe as a whole.)

They should have known from previous action that God had taken upon the earth that He detested disobedience. God moves in to thwart their pride and ambition.

Genesis 11:5. But the Lord came down to see the city and the tower which the sons of men had built.

The people acted defiantly against His commands by building a tower. This was considered an act of war, and it didn't fit into God's will. God began to go down and confounded the language, so that they could not understand one another's speech.

Genesis 11:7. "Come, let Us go down and there confuse their language, that they may not understand one another's speech."

Elohim, the triune God, interfered with man's plan of coalescing and decided to scatter them abroad throughout the face of the earth. God did this by confusing their language so that they couldn't communicate with one another, thus creating languages.

There are about 6500 distinct languages that exist in the world today. This confusion among the people by their language was called Babel. The results can be seen today. We have the United Nations, where all the different cultures and languages gather by using headphones so they can understand each other through translators. As we close the story of the tower of Babel, we are introduced here to the beginning of divisions, suspicions, and hostilities that have separated and divided the nations and the peoples of the world.

One day the Lord will restore us all to His pure language.

Zephaniah 3:9. "For then I will restore to the peoples a pure language that they all may call on the name of the Lord, to serve Him with one accord."

After the confusion at Babel, the writer revisits Shem's lineage to show us the path to Abram, which later will be known as Abraham, the father of many nations.

Another question arises from my ten-year-old: "Can I trust this genealogy?" This is not a child's disbelief in the Bible; rather, she is asking the trustworthiness of lineages recorded within Genesis. To phrase it more precisely, can we trust the Genesis genealogies?

There are many opinions on this topic from different religious denominations and teachings. Therefore, I began to pray and reread the chapter and cross-reference to other books of the Bible.

The main argument of most skeptics about the accuracy of Genesis genealogy is that it does not list months so that one will be in error when the months are added up to years. This is absolutely a standard argument. Furthermore, it is not possible for anyone to date the events of a genealogy to the absolute day and month. However, facts of the standard counting of years—correlating each event to its corresponding year—can be extracted from the Genesis genealogy.

Dr. Floyd Jones studied and considered these topics. For example, in *The Chronology of the Old Testament* (2nd printing, 1993, p. 21) Dr. Jones says: "It will be noted that a goal is that of a 'standard' chronology, not an 'absolute' chronology. As Scripture normally records only entire years for a given event and not the days and months, summing the years may yield an inaccurate total because the partial years were not included. After twelve years of examining numerous arguments, date placements, regnal data, ancient inscriptions, royal annals, eclipse calculations, etc., this researcher has concluded that any such assignment is not realistic of any chronology of prolonged duration. Even the serious notion of an absolute chronology stretches credulity and borders on the ludicrous."

One would be wise to research this further upon the work of Dr. Floyd Jones, as well as Archbishop James Ussher within his *Annals of The World.*

Although we got a preview of this in chapter 10, God begins now to focus on some of the missing names that will give us a clear lineage to the messianic conclusion. This is God's original redemptive plan from the beginning of time and creation, from the couple that He made in the garden, to the family that he rescued, to the man He designated as the father of His nations, to the virgin birth that will produce the savior of mankind. From the lineage of Shem, Jesus Christ was to be born, die, and be resurrected.

If you look closely, there are new names added to the lineage of Shem. We continue seeing the rest of Shem's genealogy within that of Nahor.

Genesis 11:24. Nahor lived twenty-nine years, and begot Terah. 25. After he begot Terah, Nahor lived one hundred and nineteen years, and begot sons and daughters. 26. Now Terah lived seventy years, and begot Abram, Nahor, and Haran.

Now we have arrived at Abram, who later became Abraham. From Abraham come numerous offspring all the way to the end of the book with Joseph. Matthew 1: 1-16 gives us the rest of the genealogy of

Shem after Abraham, all the way to Jesus, who is known as the Christ.

Matthew 1:17. So all the generations from Abraham to David are fourteen generations, from David until the captivity in Babylon are fourteen generations, and from the captivity in Babylon until the Christ are fourteen generations.

God's redemptive plan for sending His Son into the world—not to condemn it, but to save the world—is happening. We know this to be true because we see God's redemptive hope manifested in our lives. Despite the disobedience, murder, and rebellion after the wrath of the flood, God's mercy endures. God continues to look for a bride for His Son to spend the rest of eternity with.

John 3:29. He who has the bride is the bridegroom; but the friend of the bridegroom, who stands and hears him, rejoices greatly because of the bridegroom's voice. Therefore this joy of mine is fulfilled.

As we close Genesis 1 through 11, we have learned that Genesis is more than just a book of beginnings, more than a book of first things, more than the foundation of the Christian worldview; it is a book of God's blessings that are being carried out by His redemptive plan. This is the First Good News written in Genesis 3:15.

We must let the Bible be its own interpreter. This is huge when it comes to understanding Genesis 1-11. The Bible is theology—study of God—and not science or a systematic body of knowledge about one subject. The biggest reason is that the Bible has miracles that can't be explained by science.

2 Peter 3:5. For this they willfully forget: that by the word of God the heavens were of old, and the earth standing out of water and in the water, 6. by which the world that then existed perished, being flooded with water. 7. But the heavens and the earth which are now preserved by the same word are reserved for fire until the day of judgment and perdition of ungodly men.

The exegetical reading of Genesis has to be applied to understand its literary, historical, and contextual meaning. It will not align with man's ideas or philosophy. It will, however, give you God's wisdom and bottomless knowledge of how things are and ought to be.

In our search for the truth of God's intent and plan for our lives, we must not be pressured to allegorize Genesis so that it conforms to science or philosophical human ideas of old. Don't be fooled by the idea of religious neutrality. Jesus teaches us that we either gather with Him or scatter.

Matthew 12:30. He who is not with Me is against Me, and he who does not gather with Me scatters abroad.

There are men who seek to convolute the truth, and there are men who seek the truth for the glory of God.

2 Timothy 3:13. But evil men and impostors will grow worse and worse, deceiving and being deceived.

The perspicuity of the scripture is that nothing outside the Word of God reveals the truth about the scriptures. The Holy Spirit will reveal the truth about what is within the Bible, if we only ask Him through Jesus Christ our Lord and Savior.

Dear Heavenly Father, we are grateful for the knowledge that you have revealed through the story of the tower of Babel. We learned through the confusion you caused because of the disobedience of your people that you are right and just. We pray that you forgive us for our disobedience and help us to abide in your presence; through your Son, Jesus, we pray, amen.

CHAPTER 12
THE GOOD NEWS ACCORDING TO THE BELOVED APOSTLE

Son: Hey Dad, I have some good news and bad news

Tired Father: Just tell me the good news.

Son: Just the good news? Ok then, your car's airbag works perfectly.

Bereshith Bara Elohim in Hebrew means "in the beginning God". We're going back to Genesis 1:1 to point out how this has a similar approach to the gospel or good news that we are about to explore. Both begin with these sweeping words: "in the beginning".

John 1:1. In the beginning was the Word, and the Word was with God, and the Word was God. 2. He was in the beginning with God.

The redemptive story found in both Genesis and John reveals God's eternal plan. Unlike all the other synoptic gospels—synoptic means similar points of view—John is revealing the divinity of Jesus. The book of John was written by John, a close disciple of Jesus

Bishop Irenaeus gave a historical account in the beginning of the second century. Irenaeus (whose name means "peaceable") was a close student of Polycarp, who was a disciple of John. Polycarp was a student who followed John, who was himself an eyewitness of Jesus Christ.

The Gospel of John reveals a different side of Jesus. This intimate gospel reveals the deity, truth, and light of Jesus. It is proper that we put the finishing touch on our foundational book by revealing the most loving Gospel in the Bible, brought to us by the most beloved disciple of Jesus, John.

John was "the disciple whom Jesus loved". John had a special bond with Jesus because he sought Him with his whole heart. Similarly to my life, John is passionate for seeking the truth. Statistically speaking, John talks about the truth about 45 times in the Bible. His approach to the truth of Jesus comes from every angle.

John's desire is for us to believe the truth so we can have a true relationship with Jesus. His conclusions lead to the foundational beliefs of our faith, a foundation that is built through Jesus Christ our Lord and Savior.

Before we unpack John's gospel, let's find out who John really is. Although other gospels mention John by name, this book doesn't make such mention of him; rather, it only makes reference to him as "the disciple whom Jesus loved".

John 13:23. Now there was leaning on Jesus' bosom one of His disciples, whom Jesus loved.

According to Bible scholars, this book was written in Ephesus around AD 85, because that is where John was ministering to the Christian community. His message to them was that the Holy Spirit is the true Teacher.

John 14:26. But the Helper, the Holy Spirit, whom the Father will send in My name, He will teach you all things, and bring to your remembrance all things that I said to you.

Despite the delay in writing his book, John recalled all the events, and he gives insights into Jesus' words and deeds written within the gospel. John, "son of Thunder", was the son of Zebedee and Salome and the younger brother of James. Salome is mentioned a couple of times in the Gospels, such as in Mark 15:40-41.

Mark 15:40. There were also women looking on from afar, among whom were Mary Magdalene, Mary the mother of James the Less and of Joses, and Salome, 41. who also followed Him and ministered to Him when He was in Galilee, and many other women who came up with Him to Jerusalem.

According to tradition, Salome was the sister of Mary, Jesus' mother. Early Christians held that John and Jesus were cousins.

Their family conducted a fishing business in Galilee. It is worth noting that John was one of the three disciples that saw the raising of daughter of Jairus, the Transfiguration, and the agony at Gethsemane. This places John as the central eyewitness to the life and ministry of Jesus. John's gospel is the most deep and meaningful gospel that was ever written; it was considered the most sacred and holy account of Jesus.

The new message was that God's people may enter into the holy of holies, which was not accessible until now, by believing that the true Son of God has become flesh, died for our sins, and resurrected on the third day. Now He has sat down at the right hand of the throne of God.

In this Gospel, we experience God manifested in the flesh so that we may intimately know Him and feel His pain, to have a relationship with Him.

The truth is that Jesus is God in human flesh. Contrary to secular belief, this is God the everlasting, infinite, omniscient, unchanging, all-powerful, and all-knowing that has taken on human form, not to condemn but to give a way of redemption. This is the same redemptive plan that God set out from the beginning of Creation.

This is beyond Christian philosophy; this is entering the realm of deep personal relationship with the almighty God of the universe. This is the center of the Christian worldview. If you practice Christianity without having a deep personal connection with the purpose of why God became flesh and lived among us to die on the cross for our sins, then your walk is mediocre at best.

John had an intimate knowledge of Jesus as a teacher, having lived with Jesus, walked with Jesus daily, and seen Jesus suffering on the cross. John wants us to know Him like he knew Him, deeply and intimately. God is ultimately and infinitely powerful, yet He is intimately personal to each of us who choose to walk daily with Him.

How exactly did John show Jesus in his book?

John 1:1. In the beginning was the Word, and the Word was with God, and the Word was God.

This profound verse puts into perspective the true nature of Jesus as the Word of God that created the universe. This is *Memra*, a term that occurs in Targum literature with similar connotations to the Greek word *logos*, understood to mean the mind of God as revealed in creation.

Jesus is the *Logos* (a Greek word which means Word), in this context the Word of God. The Greeks understood that the world has a kind of design; it comes from *logos*, the ordering principle of all created things. The Greek word *logos* can be summarized as follows; a word is a symbol of expression of thoughts, as thought can't come to fruition without being communicated using the word. The writer is taking extra measures to provide clarity to the meaning of "Word" within the passage for those who may ask or dispute the power of the Word.

Having myself been a "witness" for a cultic movement using the same name, this explanation provides perspicuity as to the deity of Jesus, the Word of God. Jesus is God; therefore, God and the Word are one. We can rely on the faithful translation in the Bible that is used here, not that of the Jehovah Witnesses' "the new world translation of the Holy Scriptures". We should know that to understand God is to understand Him through His word as stated in Romans 11:34.

Romans 11:34. For who has known the mind of the Lord? Or who has become His counselor?

Who knows the mind of God? The mind of God can only be revealed through His Word, His *Logos*. John's revelation of the Word shows us that the Word of God is our source to know the intent, character, and essence of God.

Does it have to be the written word? The Bible shows us that God communicates through His Word even before the written word existed. Today we have the perfect Word of God within the Bible.

1 Peter 1:25. But the word of the Lord endures forever.

Now this is the word preached to you by the gospel. Within the Word, God's mind is expressed to us. John also revealed that this expression of God's mind was there from the beginning—the beginning of everything that we know of.

John 1:2. He was in the beginning with God. 3. All things were made through Him, and without Him nothing was made that was made.

Everything we know has a beginning, even angels, but the Word spans beyond everything. The Word was already there from the beginning.

John did not show the birth of Christ or the early life of Christ; he revealed the deity and eternal beginning of Christ. With no parables and fewer historical accounts, John wrote to us of the heavenly nature of Christ. The true intent of John's book is to convince all of us of the true person of Christ so that all may believe and receive eternal salvation.

John 20:31. ...but these are written that you may believe that Jesus is the Christ, the Son of God, and that believing you may have life in His name.

Moreover, John used a method that the other synoptic gospels didn't, showing the divine nature of Christ. John wrote extensively of Christ's divine works, miracles, words, titles, even prayers and worship. This demonstrates that Christ is a divine person.

John reveals Jesus as fully God, yet fully man. He was the means by which everything came into existence. Within this concept, he uses the same word expressed in Genesis, which is Light.

John 1:4. In Him was life, and the life was the light of men. 5. And the light shines in the darkness, and the darkness did not comprehend it.

John 1:9. That was the true Light which gives light to every man coming into the world.

In this profound reference to life and light, John is simply saying that life is the same as the light of men. If we were to refer to the Greek construction, it would read that the life of men was the light as the Word was God.

The Greek usage of the word "life" is categorized into three categories. They are *bios*, *psuche* or psyche, and *zoe*. Let me explain how each word is used within the context of the English word life.

Bios is the reference word that means our physical life or biological-heart-pumping existence. The psyche means our inner life within our mind, or internal satisfaction, or quality of life. *Zoe* is the most relevant usage to our understanding of God; it is also a theological term that refers to the quality of life that can only come from the true knowledge of God.

This is the eternal life that Jesus talks about. This is a divine connection. Here are some examples within the Bible.

Matthew 16:25. For whoever desires to save his life will lose it, but whoever loses his life for My sake will find it.

John 10:10. The thief does not come except to steal, and to kill, and to destroy. I have come that they may have life, and that they may have it more abundantly.

In Him, Jesus, is life. Jesus is the source of life. We can't stop there. Jesus is the source for the quality of life. One can achieve the next level through being born again to attain everlasting life, which is life eternal. This is life more abundantly through the new birth that goes on and doesn't end.

John 1:9. That was the true Light which gives light to every man coming into the world.

Let us return to the conversation that can shed light into this scripture. (Do you see what I did there?)

When you say you will be somewhere in a jiffy, you are referring to an existing unit of measurement. A jiffy is the time it takes light to travel one centimeter in a vacuum.

If we understand the science behind the light, we know it can penetrate darkness--in fact, it dispels darkness. It is fast, so fast that if you travel in a speed of light, 186,292 miles per second, you can circle the world about 7.5 times in a second. Light mainly consists of energy.

John 8:12. Then Jesus spoke to them again, saying, "I am the light of the world. He who follows Me shall not walk in darkness, but have the light of life."

Jesus came to shine light into the darkness; the darkness was the sinful nature of man. He came bearing light which is the life of men. When we accept the light, the sinful nature is dispelled. Jesus is the only eternal life source, the eternal divine light that can give eternal life to the fallen world.

John 1:5. And the light shines in the darkness, and the darkness did not comprehend it.

Although we know that light always overcomes darkness, the incomprehensible nature that darkness has to light is shown in this scripture. If we break down the word "comprehend", which is to mean understand, it would not make sense. What does John mean by understanding light? Light and darkness can't occupy the same space.

Again, we go to the Greek lexicon source and find the word *katalambano*. It means "to seize upon, take possession, or overcome". This illuminating definition is what we are looking for. Since light and darkness can't occupy the same space, the idea that light overcomes darkness puts into perspective what John is trying to tell us.

Of course, we know that the darkness refers to Satan, his demons, and all the evil acts of darkness. This becomes clear as we see in this scripture in another book from John.

1 John 1:5. This is the message which we have heard from Him and declare to you, that God is light and in Him is no darkness at all. 6. If we say that we have fellowship with Him, and walk in darkness, we lie and do not practice the truth.

Darkness and light can't occupy the same space. Jesus has come to overcome darkness and drive out Satan and his domain of darkness. We have learned that Satan introduced sin into the world and has tried to stop the messianic line of redemption several times but failed.

Satan failed to stop the Messiah through the slaughter of babies when Jesus was only a baby. Through false statements and temptations, he failed to persuade Jesus to submit to his kingdom of lies. He even tried to persuade Jesus in the garden to not do the will of the Father by rejecting the sacrifice of the cross. Darkness fails time and again. Jesus was the Light that overcame the dark power of Satan.

1 John 1:5. This is the message which we have heard from Him and declare to you, that God is light and in Him is no darkness at all.

The best news of all is that Jesus has overcome the darkness that is in the world.

John 16:33. These things I have spoken to you, that in Me you may have peace. In the world you will have tribulation; but be of good cheer, I have overcome the world."

This leads to John revealing to us one of the deepest mysteries of God: The Trinity. The triune God means God the Father, God the Son, and God the Holy Spirit are one God.

Deuteronomy 6:4. Hear, O Israel: The Lord our God, the Lord is one!

Colossians 2:9. For in Him dwells all the fullness of the Godhead bodily.

This shows us that Jesus is God in the flesh, and the Holy Spirit completes the triune God. This is where we come to understand that there is one God and yet there are three persons.

If we remember Genesis 1:2, "…the spirit of God was hovering over the face of the waters." The Holy Spirit was there from the beginning just like the Word was also there. The Trinity reveals the divinity of Christ Jesus, our Lord and Savior.

Matthew 3:16. When He had been baptized, Jesus came up immediately from the water; and behold, the heavens were opened to Him, and He saw the Spirit of God descending like a dove and alighting upon Him. 17. And suddenly a voice came from heaven, saying, "This is My beloved Son, in whom I am well pleased."

Matthew alludes to the concept of Trinity shown in this scripture, but it was John who proclaimed the divinity of Jesus. Jesus is the Word and the Word is God.

I pray that you understand what God has revealed through the Gospel of John about His divine purpose of Jesus becoming flesh and dying on the cross for the propitiation of our sins, and His resurrection reveals that you can live an eternal life through Him.

If one still lacks understanding of the inner workings of the Trinity, keep reading the Word of God and God will show Himself to you. We know that the scripture teaches us that God draws us to Christ.

John 6:44. No one can come to Me unless the Father who sent Me draws him; and I will raise him up at the last day.

When we pray and seek Him, we will find Him. It is essential to have a solid Christian worldview that includes the doctrine of the Trinity. This doctrine underlies key concepts and an understanding that is essential to our Gospel. If the threefold cord of the triune God is broken, then our Gospel is flawed.

Ecclesiastes 4:12. Though one may be overpowered by another, two can withstand him. And a threefold cord is not quickly broken.

Those who attack the Trinity do this by denying Jesus as God. This undermines not only the authority of the Word of God, but also the deity of Jesus. There are many scriptures that support the idea of the triune God, three persons but one being. (Genesis 1:26, Isaiah 48:12-16, Matthew 28:18-20, John 1:1-3,14) Orthodox Christian theology has always included the one true God as having a triune nature; this affirms the three co-equal and co-eternal persons in the Godhead.

A question may arise as to why we reference them as three "persons" in the Trinity. It is due to the characteristics shown within. Each person within the triune shows qualities of a person. These qualities could include will, intellect, morals, and even emotions. The Father, the Son, and the Holy Spirit are one God with three distinct personalities but a common-bond characteristic that binds them to each other, that is love.

The three are listed in this order because the Father is the head, then the Son, followed by the Holy Spirit. My daughter Lily asked, "How do we worship them?" The short answer is in spirit and in truth. We worship the triune God with reverence and truth with our heart, mind, and spirit. The most important aspect of worship is not to be caught up in the dynamics of God, but rather our personal relationship with Him. Each member of the Trinity should be gratified, adored, verbally glorified, and equally honored.

The revelation of God the Father, God the Son, and God the Holy Spirit within our life is seen through the love that we practice towards one another.

John 13:34. "A new commandment I give to you, that you love one another; as I have loved you, that you also love one another. 35. By this all will know that you are My disciples, if you have love for one another."

The fundamental belief of Christianity is often portrayed within the fundamental concept of five "Solas" and the Apostles' Creed. This is not just a denominational study of a particular sect of Christianity. These are stated repeatedly in the Bible as the authority of the Christian faith. The five "Solas" are as follows:

"Sola Scriptura": the scripture is the last, and infallible, court of appeal as to the truthfulness of any opinion which it addresses. The Bible is the ultimate authority of the truth and meaning of everything.

"Solus Christus": Christ paid for our salvation on the cross. Jesus lived a perfect life, always totally pleasing the Father, and never displeasing Him. When Jesus died on the cross, He was punished for sin not His own. Christ was punished as a substitute for sinners. He was punished as their substitute when He died on the cross; the perfect life and obedience of Christ is counted to God's people as they are joined to Him, and they are accepted in Christ, the Beloved, and thereby blessed with life in Him.

"Sola Fide": we receive this gift of God by faith alone. The good works which we do are a result of God's gracious work in us, and not a cause of it in any sense. The life we live is only by faith in Jesus, who loves us and gave Himself up for us.

"Sola Gratia": we are saved by grace alone. It is a gift of God, not dependent upon goodness that is within us or the works we perform for God.

"Soli De Gloria": it is all for the glory of God alone. God chooses people, provides for their redemption, draws them to Himself, and ultimately glorifies them with Himself. This is all to the praise of His glorious Name and the grace He gives.

No Christian theology is complete without acknowledging the true creed that was set by the disciples of Christ, which today we refer to as Apostles' Creed.

THE APOSTLES' CREED	BIBLE REFERENCES
I believe in God,	
(1) The Father Almighty,	1. Isaiah 44:6; 45:5
Maker of Heaven and Earth,	
(2)And in Jesus Christ,	2. Genesis 1:1; John 1:1-3; Acts 14:15
(3)His only Son,	3. Luke 2:11; John 20:28
(4) our Lord,	4. John 3:16; Proverbs 30:4
(5) who was conceived by the Holy Spirit,	5. John 20:28
(6) born of the Virgin Mary	6. Luke 1:35
(7) suffered under Pontius Pilate,	7. Luke 1:27
(8) was crucified,	8. Luke 23:23-25
(9) dead	9. John 19:20; Acts 4:10; all Gospels
(10) and buried.	10. 1 Corinthians 15:3
(11) He descended into paradise.	11. 1 Corinthians 15:4
(A) The third day	A. 1 Peter 3:18; Luke 23:43
(12) He arose from the dead,	12. 1 Corinthians 15:4
(13) He ascended into Heaven	13. 1 Corinthians 15:4
(14) and is seated at the right hand of God,	14. Mark 16:19; Luke 24:51, Acts 1:11
(15) the Father Almighty. From thence He shall come to judge the quick and the dead.	15. Mark 16:19; Hebrews 1:3
(16) I believe in the Holy Spirit,	16. 2 Timothy 4:1; John 5:22
(17) the church universal,	17. John 15:26; 16:7-8, 13-14; Acts 13:2
(18) the communion of saints,	18. Galatians 3:26-29
(19) the forgiveness of sins,	19. Revelation 19:14; Hebrews 10:25
(20)the resurrection of the body,	20. Luke 7:48
(21) and life everlasting.	21. 1 Thessalonians 4:16; John 6:39
(22)	22. John 10:28; 17:2-3

It is fitting that we end our time together with a fervent prayer to our heavenly Father.

Our heavenly Father, we come before you to lift your holy name above any other name that is the name of Jesus Christ, our Lord. We are thankful that we have received the knowledge and divine text of the Holy Scripture within this book. It gives us comfort to know that we can use the profound truth in the understanding of the Bible to guide us in our daily walk of salvation. We pray that the truth we learned will make us love you more and love each other. We know your word is true and what is written within the Bible is true. We believe with all of our hearts, minds, and souls that we can have life and more abundantly.

Father, we are grateful for the grace that you have imparted to us. Although we don't deserve it, we know that your wish is for us to be called your children, to be the heirs of the kingdom of God. As we continue to work out our salvation with fear and trembling, we can be confident that the Holy Spirit will be there to help us every step of the way. We thank you for giving us a helper to guide us to walk in your eternal truth.

We also thank you for sending your Son for the propitiation of our sins. We understand that Jesus was a gift to us because you so loved us; we will always be eternally grateful for this gift. We know that it is your wish that all come to you and receive this gift; therefore I pray, Lord, that you will work a work of saving grace in the hearts of many in the world. I pray that they will turn to the hope that lies within the Lord Jesus Christ.

Thank you for the Word of God and its clear message within the Gospel. We continue to pray for your kingdom and your glory to reign forever and ever, in Jesus' name, Amen.

CHAPTER 13
THE GOOD NEWS ACCORDING TO JESUS

Doctor Hall: I have some good news and bad news.

Patient Dan: Ok, tell me the bad news first.

Doctor Hall: Well, you have an incurable cancer.

Patient Dan: Oh my, what could be the good news?

Doctor Hall: Well, you won't have it for very long.

Now that I know Jesus is the answer, what's next? If Jesus is the answer, what is the question?

"Jesus is the answer." This catchy and popular slogan has been made prominent by authors and lecturers throughout the century. Research shows that almost every Christian denomination has adopted this theme as a way to remedy life's dilemmas.

What does it really mean to say Jesus is the answer? If Jesus is truly the answer, how do practice that in our lives? Are we obligated to share this answer with others?

In Chapter 3, we learned that Adam and Eve enjoyed a perfect fellowship with God in the Garden. When sin entered into the world because Adam disobeyed God, we lost that perfect fellowship with God, thereby bringing suffering into the world to the point of death.

Romans 5:12. Therefore, just as through one man sin entered the world, and death through sin, and thus death spread to all men, because all sinned...

Romans 6:23. For the wages of sin is death, but the gift of God is eternal life in Christ Jesus our Lord.

The death mentioned here is more than physical; it is a spiritual death. God can't fellowship with sin. It is impossible. Therefore, God began to devise a way to bring humankind back into His grace. God decided to offer a gift that is eternal life through Jesus. The redemptive plan was God's plan from the very beginning.

Genesis 3:21. Also for Adam and his wife the Lord God made tunics of skin, and clothed them.

This was the answer to Genesis 3:15, first good news, Protoevangelium, the answer which God bestowed upon the first couple. By providing a covering for Adam and Eve, sacrificing a lamb, God gifted mankind a redemption plan to reconcile man back to God.

From the very beginning of the Torah to the New Testament, God gradually reveals His salvation plan to save mankind through His only begotten Son, Jesus Christ our Savior. Jesus is the promised Redeemer; He restores the possibility of relationship with the Almighty God.

John 14:6. Jesus said to him, "I am the way, the truth, and the life. No one comes to the Father except through Me.

There it is in black and white: Jesus is the only answer. There is no other way, no other truth, and no other means to life. He is the answer to everything. Remember "Solus Christus".

Romans 5:10. For if when we were enemies we were reconciled to God through the death of His Son, much more, having been reconciled, we shall be saved by His life. 11. And not only that, but we also rejoice in God through our Lord Jesus Christ, through whom we have now received the reconciliation.

If you believe God has sent Jesus to die on the cross for the propitiation of all your sins and that He was raised from the dead days later so that you may have the power over sin and death, then you have received reconciliation; this is salvation. Jesus makes it possible for you to be forgiven and be called the children of God. Welcome to the family of God.

John 1:12. But as many as received Him, to them He gave the right to become children of God, to those who believe in His name: 13. who were born, not of blood, nor of the will of the flesh, nor of the will of man, but of God.

Now that you are saved and walking the salvation walk, you are born again like a babe in Christ.

Psalms 119:9. How can a young man cleanse his way? By taking heed according to Your word. 10. With my whole heart I have sought You; Oh, let me not wander from Your commandments! 11. Your word I have hidden in my heart, That I might not sin against You.

This is one of the earliest scriptures I have memorized. When we are a "babe in Christ", our focus is to continuously walk away from our former life. We are born again; therefore, we are a new creature with a new habit. We need to constantly meditate on the Word of God to help us turn away from sin and live for the purpose of the will of God.

1 Peter 2:2. Therefore, laying aside all malice, all deceit, hypocrisy, envy, and all evil speaking, 2. as newborn babes, desire the pure milk of the word, that you may grow thereby, 3. if indeed you have tasted that the Lord is gracious.

Now, it is time to "work out your salvation with fear and trembling".

Philippians 2:12. Therefore, my beloved, as you have always obeyed, not as in my presence only, but now much more in my absence, work out your own salvation with fear and trembling; 13. for it is God who works in you both to will and to do for His good pleasure.

Titus 2:11. For the grace of God that brings salvation has appeared to all men, 12. teaching us that, denying ungodliness and worldly lusts, we should live soberly, righteously, and godly in the present age, 13. looking for the blessed hope and glorious appearing of our great God and Savior Jesus Christ, 14. who gave Himself for us, that He might redeem us from every lawless deed and purify for Himself His own special people, zealous for good works.

When you experience the joy of salvation, you need to exercise your faith. It is similar to your daily workout (or for some of us, a 30-minute cardio every other day). It is not healthy to be spiritually passive. We need to exercise our faith in order for God to be able to work His plan within your life. We are simply a vessel for God to do His will. This is the message to all new converts; that is, exercise your faith, for it is God's will for your life.

Discipleship can be difficult if you don't have enough discipline to do it alone. In my life, I was fortunate enough to have my own personal trainer. Living with a godly family, the Olsens, God used them to train me to exercise my faith. From daily Bible reading and prayer to deep theological study of the scriptures, my faith grew stronger.

Men of faith can incentivize you to exercise your faith and increase your knowledge in theology. However, only Jesus can sustain your spiritual vigor; He is the ultimate trainer for discipleship. Even Paul conceded this when he persuaded us to follow him as he imitates God.

1 Corinthian 11:1. Imitate me, just as I also imitate Christ.

Charles Spurgeon was a great English Baptist minister who often mixed humor in his message on the pulpit. He said, "Have you no wish for others to be saved? Then you're not saved yourself, be sure of that!"

Even the atheist Penn Gillete, magician, says "I don't respect Christians who don't proselytize… How much you have to hate somebody to not proselytize." Proselytize means to convert or attempt to convert (someone) from one religion, belief, or opinion to another. In other words, to share what is going on in your life to others. This is what God's will is for your life.

1 Peter 3:15. But sanctify the Lord God in your hearts, and always be ready to give a defense to everyone who asks you a reason for the hope that is in you, with meekness and fear.

Once one is sanctified, living a godly life and exercising your faith, one is ready to give a defense to everyone who asks a reason for the hope that is in you. We do this by proselytizing; we do this by showing others around us the message of the Gospel of Jesus Christ.

Matthew 28:19. "Go therefore and make disciples of all the nations, baptizing them in the name of the Father and of the Son and of the Holy Spirit, 20. teaching them to observe all things that I have commanded you; and lo, I am with you always, even to the end of the age." Amen.

Jesus commands us to make disciples, baptize, and teach. We are to be light bearers in this dark world. Christians should disciple others to grow our faith to every corner of the world. Christians have a mission that is to spread the Gospel, the good news of God, to everyone that will hear us.

The salvation message includes the victory of Jesus over death and sin that can assure us of everlasting life in heaven forever. This is huge! This is the best message anyone could ever have; better than the message of any candidate for President in any election. This is a message of eternal hope and redemption.

Moreover, you can present this great message through your own personal testimony, which is your life. The most exciting infomercial for this message is your own walk with the Lord. A great illustration of this excitement is the story of the Samaritan woman. After believing that Jesus was the Messiah, she could not wait to share the good news.

John 4:28. The woman then left her waterpot, went her way into the city, and said to the men, 29. "Come, see a Man who told me all things that I ever did. Could this be the Christ?"

John 4:39. And many of the Samaritans of that city believed in Him because of the word of the woman who testified, "He told me all that I ever did."

Father in heaven, I pray that every person who receives this message of eternal hope will put into practice what you have command us to do, which is to share the Gospel. I pray that through the power of the Holy Spirit each of us is able to speak boldly the message of redemption of Jesus Christ dying on the cross for the propitiation of our sins and resurrecting on the third day, defeating death once and for all. Father, I know you have loved us so much that you have provided a way through your Son, Jesus, for us to have life and eternal fellowship with you now and in heaven. Thank you for that eternal hope and salvation, in Jesus' name we pray, Amen.

CHAPTER 14
THE GOOD NEWS YOU CAN SHARE

Praise Leader: I have some good news and no bad news.

Congregation: Tell us, please tell us.

Praise Leader: I have solved the hokey pokey problem.

Congregation: What is it?

Praise Leader: I've officially turned myself around.

The First Good News would not be complete without good instruction on how to do apologetics. The Apostle Peter was passionate when he shared that every Christian must be ready to share the hope that is in them. (1 Peter 3:15).

After extensive research, the conclusion I found on how to do apologetics is that the gospel is shared many ways and through various methods. Perhaps this is because humans are diverse and have different needs that can be fulfilled by the Gospel of Jesus Christ. It would be naive to think that this method or that method is the only effective method of defending the faith.

With that said, I found that there is a common thread that they all share. It will be presented within this chapter. The focus is on how to defend the faith as all truth, and at the same time observable in that it works in real life. This method is similar to that of an apologist credited in the Acknowledgements at the front of this book, but not as eloquently worded, as he is such an intellectual giant.

Using the Bible, we will follow its idea and method of implementing apologetics. It is the intention of this writer to keep it simple by keeping it at an elementary level. If you remember, it was my 10-year-old daughter that inspired me to write this book.

In apologetics, it is good to understand the question being presented, but we must know that it is the questioner that matters. With every question that is being presented, there's a presupposition behind it. In the presupposition lies the heart of the questions. We can easily separate the honest skeptic from the dishonest by simply digging through the question. Don't be afraid to say, "I don't understand what you mean."

We need to know whether or not the skeptics have a logical worldview. This can only be done through a clever method of asking questions to the questioner; be persistent but be cunning in your inquiry. You are not to interrogate the skeptic; you are to meekly address their concerns.

However, a dishonest skeptic doesn't have a logical worldview; they simply will keep giving answers or asking questions that don't follow logic or just don't make sense. When you find yourself in this situation, stop and politely show a smile, acknowledging that you know their intent.

On the other hand, after discovering that the person is an honest skeptic, this is when the Holy Spirit can work through you. One must answer the honest skeptic with good questions to find their presupposition for asking the question. Their questions will show where they stand in their worldview. It is after discovering this nugget that you will be able to give them the truth of the Word of God. You know and are ready to give them the Gospel; it is the power of God to salvation.

Upon this discovery, you can also make a determination of the entry point of the discussion. Understanding their worldview, one can start a conversation that focuses on the subject being presented. When we find the skeptic's flaws within their worldview—and there will be flaws—then we present the Gospel. We must continue to present the foundation of our faith by showing the flaws of their worldview. It is one or the other; it can't be both. The Christian worldview can't be built within the foundation of man's worldview.

Luke 16:13. "No servant can serve two masters; for either he will hate the one and love the other, or else he will be loyal to the one and despise the other. You cannot serve God and mammon."

Building a Christian worldview requires pragmatism, an approach that assesses the truth of the meaning of theories or beliefs in terms of the success of their practical application; it is shown through our personal testimony. This is why Peter said "but sanctify the Lord your God in your heart…" first because without it our message is ineffective. It is only through our true conversion in Christ that the apologetics begins.

Remember the story of the Samaritan woman in John chapter 4; she was a true skeptic because her questions reflected a genuine need in her life. If you are not familiar with the story, please read it. There is a wealth of information on the tactics of Christian apologetics.

We need Christians that can defend their faith by their own personal testimony, not merely heard but seen. We need to learn to listen to the questioner more deeply than the question; then we can get to the heart of the matter. The truth of the Gospel deals with matters of the heart, not just winning an intellectual argument.

Christian apologetics are intentional and purposeful. They must always present their argument with a great amount of prayer and intercession. The game plan is to present the hope that is already inside of you using tactics that are within the Word of God.

Presenting the hope that is in you should not be intimidating to any Christians. Yet many Christians find it difficult to share the Gospel that they already believe. The reason could be that they are not grounded in the Christian worldview. However, the good news is that the Bible offers us the tools we need to do apologetics, to defend the faith. If you're willing to learn some basic principles that the Bible lays out, then you too could be effective in apologetics.

When God presents an opportunity to engage in a conversation to defend your faith, first you must ask God for wisdom and pray. A quick prayer will put your mind into a godly mode; this will guard your mind from getting sidetracked into engaging in scientific arguments or nuances.

Do not argue with the first question from the questioner. Ask questions until you get a worldview from the questioner.

Once you arrive at the matter of the heart issue, then present a scripture to signify where you stand. Everyone has a worldview; don't be misled when they tell you that they don't. Only the disingenuous skeptic is the one that doesn't want to present their worldview; in this case your conversation would cease; just pray for them.

Whenever you are confronted with a genuine skeptic like the Samaritan woman, you can present how your worldview differs from theirs. Non-Christian worldviews will have internal defects because their foundation is not the Bible. They will consist of irrational and illogical lines of reasoning to arrive at their conclusions. You must find the flaw; it is not difficult to find it with clever questioning technique.

Proverbs 1:7. The fear of the Lord is the beginning of knowledge, But fools despise wisdom and instruction.

The Word of God is the foundation of your Christian worldview. Anyone who undermines the authority of the Word of God will be proven false, and their worldview will be flawed. We should never let things outside the Word of God be added to prove the meaning within; this is malpractice. The Bible is the root of all essential knowledge.

How do we get to the heart of the matter? God made the human mind to think rationally; if we can ask the right questions to unpack their motives then we can get to the heart of the matter. These are questions such as, "Can you tell me what you mean by that?" or, "How do you know that?" These types of questions will propel you to get to their worldview. Keep in mind that you are trying to get to the heart of the matter; don't get sidetracked.

The Bible offers another strategy that we can use to unpack the skeptic's worldview. This advice comes from the wisest person that existed, none other than King Solomon, son of David. He gave us a couple of verses that are profound and prove beneficial in the scope of defending our faith. He also gave us a strategy to expose the flaws within the skeptic's worldview.

Proverbs 26:4. Do not answer a fool according to his folly, Lest you also be like him.

"A fool" is the Bible's way of describing anyone who doesn't have a Christian worldview. Therefore, this is not an exercise in name-calling, nor should we ever engage in any argument that attacks a person's character. Do not engage in an ad hominem, a reaction directed against a person and not the idea they are conveying.

Whenever a person rejects the foundational truth of the Word of God, the unbeliever is "foolish" in the Hebrew meaning of the word. The idea is to not follow the fool's line of reasoning or their illogical pattern to arrive at their conclusion. It is a well of foolishness that you will find yourself drowning in. The fool will try to disarm you by setting terms to undermine the authority of the Word of God.

They will suggest you do not use the Bible to support your argument; but this term can never be agreed upon. The Bible is the foundation of our belief; it is our sword of truth. Do not let skeptics take that away from you; otherwise, you will be a fool like he is.

Another suggestion of skeptics may be that you are not allowed to present any miracles of the Bible as legitimate explanations because they are not scientific. The short answer is that God performs miracles even from the beginning of time in Genesis 1:1.

According to the next verse in Proverbs, we should also not fall into the trap of "answering a fool according to his folly" or else we will be just like him.

Proverbs 26:5 Answer a fool according to his folly, Lest he be wise in his own eyes.

Do not be confused by this second proverb from King Solomon; he is not contradicting himself. This is an instruction provided by the wise king to show us how to answer the fool. The concept here is to present our Christian worldview to disprove their flawed and inconsistent belief system. This is where we answer them to show that their worldview doesn't have a firm foundation.

The Christian worldview is firmly grounded upon the foundation of the Word of God. We can share our defense of the faith with meekness and trembling. After listening to their worldview, not necessarily agreeing, then we can gently guide them to show that it led to an absurd conclusion. When we show the absurdity of their worldview by turning the mirror on them, they can clearly see that without the Bible their foundation is not solid. Their philosophy will ultimately fail.

There are many apologists that have endorsed this powerful method in different forms and techniques. These tools are used by great evangelists and teachers such as Greg Koukl, Frank Turek, Ken Ham, and Jason Lisle. It was the great Isaac Newton in 1675 who said, "If I have seen further it is by standing on the shoulders of Giants." This is absolutely a premise of this book. Without these great teachers, this writer will not have a complete knowledge of the truth. The Word of God offers the foundation, but these intellectual giants in the Christian world provided me the perspicuity of the writing within the scriptures.

It is by the grace of God through Jesus Christ our Lord that I am able to compile my thoughts and put them into this book. Let us thank the Heavenly Father for this time we have had together.

Our Heavenly Father, we are thankful for the Word of God that was written for our learning. Teach me today, in the power of your Holy Spirit, the truths that you would have me learn.

Father, I know that man shall not live by bread alone, but by every word that proceeds out of the mouth of God. Feed me on your Word, I pray, and make me hungry for the living bread that came down from heaven, the heavenly Bread of Life and the true living water, who alone can bring us into our eternal salvation.

I pray that the Holy Spirit will open our mind today as we read and study the Word of God. Let our mind be willing to be led into the truth within your Word. Please grant me a willing heart and the opportunity to share with others the Gospel of Jesus

Christ because it is the power to change lives. In Jesus' name, I pray, amen.